DISDBIS

Dissertationen zu Datenbanken und Informationssystemen

Mit Unterstützung des Fachausschusses 2.5 "Rechnergestützte Informationssysteme" der Gesellschaft für Informatik e.V. herausgegeben von

H.-J. Appelrath, Oldenburg
R. Bayer, München
W. Benn, Chemnitz
A.B. Cremers, Bonn
P. Dadam, Ulm
K.R. Dittrich, Zürich
H.-D. Ehrich, Braunschweig
G. Engels, Paderborn
B. Freitag, Passau
J.-C. Freytag, Berlin
N. Fuhr, Dortmund
G. Gottlob, Wien
O. Günther, Berlin
U. Güntzer, Tübingen
H. Güting, Hagen
T. Härder, Kaiserslautern
A. Heuer, Rostock
K. Hinrichs, Münster
S. Jablonski, Erlangen
M. Jarke, Aachen
P. Kandzia, Kiel
G. Kappel, Linz
U. Kelter, Siegen
A. Kemper, Passau
K. Küspert, Jena
W. Lamersdorf, Hamburg
G. Lausen, Freiburg
V. Linnemann, Lübeck
U. Lipeck, Hannover

P. Lockemann, Karlsruhe
R. Manthey, Bonn
H.C. Mayr, Klagenfurt
K. Meyer-Wegener, Dresden
B. Mitschang, Stuttgart
E. Neuhold, Darmstadt
H. Noltemeier, Würzburg
E. Rahm, Leipzig
A. Reuter, Bruchsal
G. Saake, Magdeburg
H.-J. Schek, Zürich
G. Schlageter, Hagen
J. Schmidt, Hamburg
M. Scholl, Konstanz
M. Schrefl, Linz
H. Schweppe, Berlin
B. Seeger, Marburg
R. Studer, Karlsruhe
B. Thalheim, Cottbus
R. Unland, Essen
G. Vossen, Münster
B. Walter, Trier
H. Weber, Berlin
H. Wedekind, Erlangen
L. Wegner, Kassel
G. Weikum, Saarbrücken
P. Widmayer, Zürich
R. Zicari, Frankfurt

Building Integrative Enterprise Knowledge Portals with Semantic Web Technologies

Torsten Priebe

Torsten Priebe
Hemauerstraße 15
D-93047 Regensburg
Germany
E-mail: tp@priebe-it.de

Dissertation zur Erlangung des Grades eines
Doktors der Wirtschaftswissenschaft
Eingereicht an der Wirtschaftswissenschaftlichen
Fakultät der Universität Regensburg

Vorgelegt von: Dipl.-Wirt.Inf. Torsten Priebe

Berichterstatter:
Prof. Dr. Günther Pernul
Prof. Dr. Hannes Federrath

Tag der Disputation: 6. Juli 2005

Die Deutsche Bibliothek lists this publication in the *Deutsche Nationalbibliografie*;
detailed bibliographic data is available on the Internet at
http://dnb.ddb.de.

"infix" is a joint imprint of Akademische Verlagsgesellschaft Aka GmbH and IOS Press
BV (Amsterdam)

Reproduced from PDF supplied by the author
Printing and Binding: Hundt Druck GmbH, Köln
Printed in Germany

ISSN 0949-0183
ISBN 3-89838-492-6
ISBN 1-58603-584-3

Foreword

Today, finding the appropriate information or even locating all the potential information sources is often more a question of luck than anything else. Traditional approaches for information management and retrieval do not adequately address the current flooding. Users are often left with thousands of search results and due to poor ranking have to filter the results manually. Additionally, search mechanisms are usually not coupled with application systems used for daily business tasks, i.e. they rely on the users to formulate search queries manually rather than proactively searching for relevant information.

The recent concept of web-based portals proves to be a very suitable platform for knowledge management. Knowledge portals are flexible, can be personalized, and thus intuitively understood by the users. They are easy to use and may deliver almost any kind of content or application functionality on a single integrated user interface. There are several features a successful portal platform must provide. Among the most important ones are the potential of integrating different sources, the categorization of resources and intelligent search capabilities, easy content publication and distribution, support of user collaboration, and easy handling through personalization, and flexible presentation features. However, considering the commercially available products, some of the characteristics are unfortunately still only supported at a very limited level today.

The following research work on "Building Integrative Enterprise Knowledge Portals with Semantic Web Technologies" addresses the gap between the demands and potentials on the one hand and the state of development and technology in the currently commercially available portal platforms on the other hand by making contributions in three major areas:

- *Semantic metadata:* Metadata based on taxonomies and organization-wide ontologies is the key to improving both search and integration facilities of knowledge portals. The task of producing semantic metadata on a large scale is however time consuming and costly. The solution proposed in this work is a semi-automatic approach for the annotation of textual documents. Technologies originally developed for the Semantic Web are used for metadata representation and reasoning.

- *Search:* A global search mechanism involving heterogeneous information sources is required. There are new requirements for searching ontology-based metadata which are considered by adapting a similarity-based information retrieval approach.

- *Integration:* A true integration of external applications requires a generic semantics-aware inter-portlet communication mechanism. The solution provided supports the integration process by incorporating the context the users are in when interacting with the portal. Again, Semantic Web technologies are used to represent the context and to transport (and translate) it among the portlets.

This book describes state-of-the-art achievements in a wide range of topics, such as enterprise knowledge portals, Semantic Web and metadata technologies, information retrieval and search strategies. Its focus is mainly on the technical issues. The research presented follows a design research methodology which also led to a publicly available comprehensive prototype implementation. The book is recommended to readers who are interested in the research contributions, but also to those looking for a comprehensive summary of the state-of-the-art of the underlying technologies.

Prof. Dr. Günther Pernul
Regensburg, Germany

Preface

When Tim Berners-Lee introduced his idea of the Semantic Web, he envisioned software agents that will act on behalf of humans and completely change the way we live our lives. An agent on the Internet could automatically make an appointment with a doctor, find a suitable restaurant, etc. While this vision is far from becoming reality, the specifications within the Semantic Web Initiative of the Word Wide Web Consortium provide, however, standardization and interoperability for a number of technologies that are already today very well applicable in an enterprise setting. This especially applies to the area of knowledge management, which is so far characterized by rather isolated and proprietary solutions. A major challenge of today's information systems is to provide employees with the right information at the right time. This involves structured information stored in databases accessible through operational and analytical application systems as well as unstructured (often textual) documents. The integration of both types of information has been subject to quite some research, however, the results are so far unsatisfying, mainly due to the lack of interoperability of the technologies used.

Enterprise portals have become the de-facto standard for web application delivery. In fact, they are more and more seen as a "standard workplace" for employees due to their ability to combine different applications and information sources on a single web-based user interface. With the convergence of portal and knowledge management technology, enterprise knowledge portals are the solution of choice for providing integrated access to structured and unstructured information. This work analyzes how Semantic Web technologies can help building integrative enterprise knowledge portals. Three main areas of interest are identified: content and structure management, global searching, and the integration of external content and applications. For these three areas the state-of-the-art as well as novel proposals are presented.

I am aware that this opens up a rather broad research arena. Actually, the research work presented in the following started off with the motivation of integrating a business intelligence (OLAP) system with an information retrieval (IR) system that searches for related documents. This is still the main scenario for the presented proposal. However, it turned out that the use of portal and Semantic Web technologies allows for a rather generic approach that can also be applied to other scenarios. Hence, the challenging goal of this work is to develop a generic framework for semantic enterprise portals without losing the focus for providing a viable solution to the mentioned OLAP/IR integration issue.

Of course, it would have been impossible to reach this goal without the support from many other people. First of all, I would like to thank my advisor Günther Pernul who gave me the necessary freedom for creativity while still now and then taking me back to the ground of research reality. ;-) He also gave me the invaluable chance to discuss my research ideas with a broad community at a number of scientific conferences. Many thanks also go to my co-advisor Hannes Federrath who without being too deeply involved in my research still provided me with very valuable feedback.

Secondly, I thank my colleagues and friends at the department in Regensburg, namely Wolfgang Dobmeier, Jörg Gilberg, Björn Muschall, and Christian Schläger who were always open for fruitful discussions and went through the hassle of proofreading this work. In addition,

I would particularly like to thank Christine Kiss from the Technical University of Munich, Thomas Hädrich from the Martin-Luther-University Halle-Wittenberg, Karlheinz Morgenroth from the University of Bamberg, and Peter Bednar and Jan Paralic from the Technical University of Kosice, Slovakia for their collaboration.

Last but not least, I owe thanks to our students in Regensburg who contributed to this work with their projects, seminar papers, and master theses. Again, without all this help, this work would not have been possible.

Torsten Priebe
Regensburg, Germany

Contents

List of Figures

List of Tables

Acronyms

AAI	Authentication and Authorization Infrastructure
ABAC	Attribute-based Access Control
AOM	(SAP) Application Object Model
API	Application Programming Interface
ASF	Apache Software Foundation[1]
B2B	Business-to-Business
B2C	Business-to-Consumer
B2E	Business-to-Employee
BI	Business Intelligence
BPR	Business Process Reengineering
BW	(SAP) Business Warehouse
C2A	(IBM) Click-to-Action
CDCQ-CR	Crisp Data, Crisp Query, Crisp Result
CDCQ-FR	Crisp Data, Crisp Query, Fuzzy Result
CDFQ-FR	Crisp Data, Fuzzy Query, Fuzzy Result
CMS	Content Management System
CRM	Customer Relationship Management
DECOR	Delivery of Context-sensitive Organisational Knowledge [ABN+01]
DL	Description Logics
DMS	Document Management System
DQP	(Microsoft) Distributed Query Processor
DR	Data Retrieval
EAI	Enterprise Application Integration
EPCF	(SAP) Enterprise Portal Client Framework
ERP	Enterprise Resource Planning
FDFQ-FR	Fuzzy Data, Fuzzy Query, Fuzzy Result
GIS	Geographical Information System
GOAL	Geographical Information Online Analysis [KMM00]
HTML	Hypertext Markup Language
HTTP	Hypertext Transfer Protocol
IETF	Internet Engineering Task Force[2]
IFRAME	Inline Frame
INWISS	Integrative Enteprise Knowledge Portal ("Integratives Wissensportal")
IR	Information Retrieval
IS	Information System(s)
ISO	International Organization for Standardization[3]

---

[1] http://www.apache.org
[2] http://www.ietf.org
[3] http://www.iso.org

IT	Information Technology
J2EE	Java 2 Enterprise Edition
JBowl	Java Text Mining and Retrieval Library (Java Bag of Words Library)[4]
JCP	Java Community Process[5]
JDBC	Java Database Connectivity
JSP	Java Server Pages
JSR	Java Specification Request
KM	Knowledge Management
KMS	Knowledge Management System
LDAP	Lightweight Directory Access Protocol
MIME	Multipurpose Internet Mail Extensions
MVC	Model View Controller
NITF	News Industry Text Format
NLP	Natural Language Processing
OASIS	Organization for the Advancement of Structured Information Standards[6]
OCS	Open Content Syndication
ODBC	Open Database Connectivity
OLAP	Online Analytical Processing
OWL	Web Ontology Language [W3C04a]
OWLIR	OWL and Information Retrieval [SFJ+02]
PDF	Portable Document Format
PLM	Product Lifecycle Management
POKER	Process Oriented Knowledge Delivery [Fen02]
PreBIS	Pre-Built Information Space [BH05]
PRISM	Publishing Requirement for Industry Standard Markup
RDF	Resource Description Framework [W3C04d]
RDFS	RDF Schema [W3C04c]
RDQL	RDF Data Query Language
RF	(SAP) Repository Framework
RFC	Request for Comment
RM	(SAP) Repository Manager
RQL	RDF Query Language
RSS	RDF Site Summary, Really Simple Syndication, Rich Site Summary
RuleML	Rule Markup Language[7]
SEAL	Semantic Portal [SMS+01]
SeRQL	Sesame RDF Query Language
SOAP	Simple Object Access Protocol
SRM	Supplier Relationship Management
SPARQL	Simple Protocol and RDF Query Language [W3C05]
SQL	Structured Query Language
SVD	Singular Value Decomposition
SWRL	Semantic Web Rule Language [DAM03]
UDDI	Universal Description, Discovery, and Integration [OAS02]
UML	Unified Modeling Language
UOM	(SAP) Unified Object Model

[4]http://webocrat.fei.tuke.sk/jbowl/
[5]http://www.jcp.org
[6]http://www.oasis-open.org
[7]http://www.ruleml.org

URI	Uniform Resource Identifier
URL	Uniform Resource Locator
VSM	Vector Space Model
W3C	World Wide Web Consortium[8]
WebDAV	Web-based Distributed Authoring and Versioning
WCMS	Web Content Management System
WSDL	Web Service Definition Language
WSIA	Web Services for Interactive Applications
WSRP	Web Services for Remote Portlets [OAS03]
WSRP4J	WSRP for Java[9]
WWW	World Wide Web
XML	Extensible Markup Language
XSL	Extensible Stylesheet Language
XSLT	XSL Transformations

---

[8]http://www.w3.org
[9]http://ws.apache.org/wsrp4j/

Chapter 1

Introduction

A major challenge of today's information systems is to provide employees with the right information at the right time [Ums90]. This task is addressed by knowledge management systems (KMS) that deal with the efficient creation and distribution of knowledge within enterprises. Knowledge appears as information in structured databases accessible through operational and analytical application systems as well as unstructured documents (office documents, emails, etc.) managed by document or content management systems (or simply stored on file servers). The integration of both types of information has been subject to quite some research, however, the results are so far unsatisfying. In order to be usable as knowledge, information needs to be meaningfully embedded in a context through experience, communication, or inference [Mai04]. This means that it is desirable to provide employees with precisely the information they need for fulfilling their current business tasks. Regular KMS are isolated tools that have evolved from the tradition of data and information management. They thus have only limited capabilities for supporting an information supply that meets this demand.

Ideally, enterprise knowledge portals provide a platform with advanced knowledge services for publication, discovery, collaboration, and learning, which brings together the various heterogeneous information sources of an organization. Using web-based technologies, portal systems allow combining different portal components (so-called portlets) side by side on a single portal webpage, representing different information sources and applications (see chapter 3). Hence, they constitute a solid basis for an efficient, integrated knowledge supply. However, in today's portal systems there is only little interaction between those portlets, which limits the possibilities for "true" integration [PP03].

Semantic Web technologies [BLHL01] aim at structuring, describing, translating, reasoning about, and securely accessing metadata and provide promising starting points for developing semantic information systems. The Resource Description Framework (RDF) and the Web Ontology Language (OWL) have evolved as standards from the Semantic Web Initiative of the Word Wide Web Consortium [W3C04d, W3C04c, W3C04a] (see chapter 4). Ontologies help to represent the semantics of the organizational knowledge base and link knowledge elements from multiple systems on a semantic level.

The research goal of this work is to analyze how Semantic Web technologies can help building enterprise knowledge portals that provide a truly integrated and situational access to structured and unstructured information as well as application functionality. Three main areas of interest are identified: content and structure management, global searching, and the integration of external content and applications. For these three areas the state-of-the-art as well as novel proposals are presented. The use of Semantic Web technologies in enterprise knowledge portals has also been proposed in other works, such as OntoViews [MHSV04], ODESwE [CGPLC+03], and SEAL [SMS+01]. They however focus on the first area, content and structure management, address global searching only in part, and completely overlook the third area, the semantic integration of external applications, which is is inevitable for drawing the bridge between unstructured and structured information. Our proposal in this area, the context-based portlet integation approach presented in chapter 10, is the main contribution of this work. It has been implemented and evaluated within the INWISS knowledge portal prototype[1] [Pri04], presented in chapter 11.

1.1   Research Questions

The applicability of Semantic Web technologies for integrating structured and unstructured information in enterprises opens up a number of research questions. The most important ones that are addressed in this work are sketched in the following:

- *What are the requirements for providing an integrated, situational access to structured and unstructured information in enterprises?*
  Before addressing concrete technical issues we need to carefully define the goals we want to achieve, i.e. we need to identify the actual problem we are trying to solve. Chapter 2 addresses the motivation and problem definition in detail.

- *Which are the (technical) features needed for this purpose?*
  After the problem has been identified, the required technical features for the solution need to be derived. This question is also addressed in chapter 2.

- *Which is the current (state-of-practice) solution of choice?*
  Before suggesting improvements, the current state-of-practice needs to be analyzed. In chapter 3 enterprise knowledge portals are identified as the current solution of choice with content and structure management, global searching, and the integration of external applications as major fields of interest for our problem area.

- *Can content and structure management in enterprise knowledge portals be improved?*
  The main research question is the applicability of Semantic Web technologies for improving the current state-of-the-art. The first area, content and structure management, is addressed in chapter 5, which analyzes the role of metadata and proposes the use of a taxonomy for navigation and an ontology for searching and contextualization.

- *How can the annotation of documents with semantic metadata be accomplished?*
  The use of semantic metadata requires an annotation of (textual) documents, which normally has to be done manually. This extra effort for users creates a risk for the acceptance of the system. A semi-automatic approach is sketched in chapter 6.

- *Can global searching in enterprise knowledge portals be improved?*
  The second area of interest, global searching, is addressed in chapter 7. Again, the use of ontology-based metadata is proposed as it can help overcome heterogeneity issues of the different sources.

- *How can a fuzzy search on ontology-based metadata be realized?*
  The use of an ontology for document annotation poses new requirements to search engines. A similarity-based information retrieval approach for ontology-based metadata is presented in chapter 8.

---

[1]http://www.inwiss.org

- *Can the integration of external applications into portals be improved?*
  The third area, the integration of external applications (for accessing structured data and for contextualization), is addressed in chapter 9. It reveals that "true" integration requires a generic, semantics-aware inter-portlet communication mechanism.

- *How can a generic, semantics-aware inter-portlet communication mechanism be realized in portal systems?*
  A context-based portlet integration approach that uses Semantic Web technologies for representing the user context is presented in chapter 10. This proposal is the main contribution of this work.

1.2 Research Method

Research methodology is a largely discussed topic in the Information Systems (IS) community, particularly in the Anglo-American world. Research methods can be classified in various ways, however one of the most common distinctions is between qualitative and quantitative research methods [Cre94]:

- *Quantitative research* methods were originally developed in natural sciences to study natural phenomena. Examples of quantitative methods that are now also well accepted in social sciences include survey methods, laboratory experiments, formal methods (e.g., econometrics), and numerical methods such as mathematical modeling. Quantitative research is also known as following a positivist perspective [SGB04].

- *Qualitative research* methods were developed in social sciences to enable researchers to study social and cultural phenomena. Examples of qualitative methods are action research, case study research, and ethnography. Qualitative data sources include observations and participant observations (fieldwork), interviews and questionnaires, documents and texts, and the researcher's impressions and reactions (interpretive perspective) [Mye97].

This work, however, follows a third paradigm complementing the above two perspectives, which has its roots mainly in Engineering and Computer Science disciplines and is often referred to as *design research*. Design research in IS involves the analysis of the use and performance of designed artifacts to understand, explain, and very frequently improve the behavior of information systems. Such artifacts include algorithms, human/computer interfaces, and system design methodologies or languages [VK04]. Following a number of years of a general shift in IS research away from technological to managerial and organizational issues, an increasing number of observers are calling for a return to an exploration of the "IT" that underlies all IS research [OI01].

Vaishnavi & Kuechler [VK04] give a comprehensive discussion of the question whether (and why) design research can be considered an appropriate technique for conducting research in Information Systems; the skeptical reader is pointed to their excellent survey. They also discuss how design research can be distinguished from regular (state-of-practice) design. In a typical industry design effort it is generally desirable to produce a new product using state-of-practice application of state-of-practice techniques and readily available components, i.e. most design efforts in industry try to minimize the risk of the design effort. The risks are however precisely the targets of design research efforts, i.e. design research can be distinguished by the intellectual risk and the number of unknowns in the proposed design which produce interesting new knowledge (for the community of interest) when successfully accomplished.

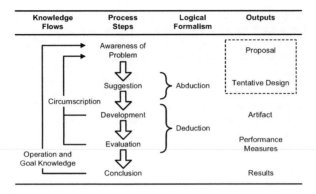

Figure 1.1: General methodology of design research (adapted from [VK04])

1.2.1 Design Research Methodology

Takeda et al. [TVTY90] have analyzed the reasoning that occurs in a general design cycle. Based on their findings Vaishnavi & Kuechler [VK04] present the process steps and outputs of design research as illustrated in figure 1.1.

In this model all design begins with the *awareness of a problem*. Design research is sometimes called "improvement research" which emphasizes its problem-solving/performance-improving nature. *Suggestions* for a problem solution are abductively drawn from the existing knowledge/theory base for the problem area [Pie31]. An attempt to implement an artifact according to the suggested solution is performed next, shown as *development* in the diagram. Partially or fully successful implementations are then *evaluated* (according to the functional specification implicit or explicit in the suggestion). Development, evaluation, and further suggestion are often iteratively performed in the course of the research (design) effort. *Conclusion* indicates the termination of a specific design project.

The basis of the iteration, the flow from partial completion of the cycle back to the awareness of the problem, is indicated by the *circumscription* arrow. The circumscription process is especially important for understanding design research because it generates knowledge that could only be gained from the specific act of construction. The design researcher learns or discovers when things do not work "according to theory". This happens many times not due to a misunderstanding of the theory, but due to the necessarily incomplete nature of any knowledge base [VK04].

In the following, the individual phases of a design research effort are described in more detail and aligned with the chapters of this work.

Awareness of Problem

The awareness of an interesting problem may come from multiple sources, e.g., new developments in industry or in a reference discipline. Reading in an allied discipline may also provide the opportunity for application of new findings to the researcher's field. The output of this phase is a proposal, formal or informal, for a new research effort [VK04].

The problem that is tackled within this work is the unsatisfying integration of structured and unstructured information and its contextualization in enterprises. The motivation and technical requirements are analyzed in chapter 2. After identifying enterprise knowledge portals as the solution of choice in chapter 3, the coarse idea (proposal) of this work is that Semantic Web technologies can eliminate (or at least diminish) remaining deficiencies. An overview on Semantic Web technologies is given in chapter 4.

Suggestion

The suggestion phase follows immediately behind the proposal and is intimately connected with it as the dotted line around proposal and tentative design (the output of the suggestion phase) in figure 1.1 indicates. If after consideration of an interesting problem a tentative design does not present itself to the researcher, the proposal will be set aside. Suggestion is the essential creative step of a design research effort where new functionality is envisioned based on a novel configuration of either existing or new and existing elements [VK04].

This is also the case for this work. Existing elements are disussed as state-of-the-art in chapters 5, 7, and 9; new elements are proposed in chapters 6, 8, and 10.

Development

The tentative design is implemented in this phase. The techniques for implementation will of course vary depending on the artifact to be constructed. For example, an algorithm may require construction of a formal proof, a software system embodying novel assumptions about human cognition will require software development. The implementation itself can be very straightforward and does not need to involve novelty beyond the state-of-practice; the novelty is primarily in the design, not the construction of the artifact [VK04].

Chapter 11 presents the prototypical implementation of the design carried out within this work. As for any prototype the focus of the development was to provide a proof-of-concept rather than a final product.

Evaluation

Once constructed, the artifact is evaluated according to criteria that are implicitly or explicitly stated in the proposal (awareness of problem phase). Deviations from expectations, both quantitative and qualitative, are noted and tentatively explained. In design research, initial hypothesis concerning the behavior of the artifact are rarely completely borne out. Instead, the evaluation results and additional information gained in the construction and running of the artifact are fed back to another round of suggestion (see the circumscription arrows of figure 1.1). The explanatory hypotheses, which are quite broad, are rarely discarded but rather modified to be in accordance with the new observations. This suggests a new design, frequently preceded by new library research in directions suggested by deviations from theoretical performance [VK04].

The prototype (and hence the design) of this work is also evaluated within chapter 11. Further suggestions for improvement are given in chapter 12.

Conclusion

This is the final phase of a specific design research effort. At some point, although there might still be minor deviations in the behavior of the artifact from the hypothetical predictions, the results are judged to be good enough. Not only are the results of the effort consolidated and written up at this phase, but the knowledge gained in the effort is frequently categorized as either firm facts that have been learned and can be repeatedly applied or as behavior that can be

Table 1.1: Philosophical assumptions of the three research perspectives [VK04]

	Positivist	Interpretive	Design
Ontology	A single reality, knowable, probabilistic	Multiple realities, socially constructed	Multiple, contextually situated alternative world states, socio-technologically enabled
Epistemology	Objective, dispassionate, detached observer of truth	Subjective, i.e. values and knowledge emerge from the researcher-participant interaction	Knowing through making: objectively constrained construction within a context, iterative circumscription reveals meaning
Methodology	Observation, quantitative, statistical	Participation, qualitative, hermeneutical, dialectical	Developmental, measure artifactual impacts on the composite system

repeatably invoked or as anomalous behavior that may serve as the subject of further research [VK04].

A conclusion for the research presented in this work is given in chapter 13, recalling and answering the above research questions from section 1.1.

1.2.2 Philosophical Grounding

Finally, without stressing the details, we would like to shortly present the philosophical grounding of design research as applied in this work (i.e. the ontological and epistemological assumptions[2]). Vaishnavi & Kuechler [VK04] summarize the philosophical assumptions of the three research paradigms as shown in table 1.1.

The assumptions of design research are unique. First, neither the ontology nor the epistemology of the paradigm is derivable from any other. Second, ontological and epistemological viewpoints shift in design research as the project runs through circumscription cycles as depicted in figure 1.1. This iteration is similar to but more radical than the hermeneutic processes used in some interpretive (qualitative) research.

Design research by definition changes the world through the introduction of novel artifacts. Thus, design researchers are comfortable with alternative world states. The obvious contrast is with positivist ontology (of quantitative researchers) where a single, given composite socio-technical system is the typical unit of analysis; even the problem statement is subject to revision as a design research effort proceeds. However, the multiple world states of the design researcher are not the same as the multiple realities of the interpretive researcher. The abductive phase of design research (see figure 1.1) in which physical laws are tentatively composed into a configuration that will produce an artifact with the intended problem solving functionality demands a natural-science-like belief in a single, fixed grounding reality.

Epistemologically, the design researcher knows that a piece of information is factual and what that information means through the process of construction/circumscription. An artifact is constructed; its behavior is the result of interactions between components. Descriptions of the interactions are information and to the degree the artifact behaves predictably the information is

___

[2]*Ontology* in this context is the study that describes the nature of reality: for example, what is real and what is not, what is fundamental and what is derivative. *Epistemology* is the study that explores the nature of knowledge: for example, on what does knowledge depend and how can we be certain of what we know [VK04].

true. Its meaning is precisely the functionality it enables in the composite system (artifact and user); it means what it does. The design researcher is thus a pragmatist [Pie31]. The dependence on a predictably functioning artifact (instrument) gives design research an epistemology that resembles that of natural-science research more closely than that of either positivist or interpretive research.

1.3 Chapter Structure

The chapter structure of this work is depicted in figure 1.2. The remainder is structured in three parts: Part I motivates the topic from a knowledge management perspective and presents enterprise knowledge portals and Semantic Web technologies as fundamentals. Part II is the main part of this work and discusses the three areas of interest: metadata for content and structure management, global searching, and the integration of external content and applications. It comprises chapters covering the state-of-the-art and proposed extensions in an alternating fashion. This leads to rather short chapters, but provides a "fast track" through this work for readers interested in an overview of the state-of-the-art, rather than novel scientific proposals by skipping the right-hand part of figure 1.2. On the other hand, researchers with good background knowledge in the field are pointed directly to chapters 6, 8, 10, and 11 (shown in italic in the figure) for the scientific contribution of this work. Finally, part III evaluates the proposals by presenting the INWISS prototype and discusses possible future directions, followed by a summary and conclusion.

Part I: Motivation and Fundamentals

Chapter 2 motivates the topic from the angle of knowledge management and discusses related work on context-based information retrieval. Chapter 3 gives an overview on enterprise knowledge portals, presenting a reference architecture as well as the role of portlets. Among others, content and structure management, global searching, and the integration of external content and applications are identified as core functionalities of enterprise knowledge portals. An overview on Semantic Web technologies is given in chapter 4. Their use within the mentioned areas of enterprise knowledge portals is discussed in part II.

Part II: State-of-the-Art and Proposed Extensions

This is the main part of this work. Chapters 5, 7, and 9 cover the state-of-the-art; new proposals are presented in chapters 6, 8, and 10.

The role of metadata for content and structure management is discussed in chapter 5; it identifies the annotation of unstructured documents with semantic metadata as an open issue. An approach for a semi-automatic annotation of text documents based on text mining and information extraction is proposed as a solution to this issue in chapter 6.

Approaches for global searching in enterprise knowledge portals are discussed in chapter 7. Existing search engines mainly use fulltext keywords; the use of ontolgy-based metadata opens up new possibilities for semantic searching, requiring however an adaption of existing information retrieval techniques. Hence, a similarity-based information retrieval approach on ontology-based metadata is proposed in chapter 8.

Finally, the integration of external content and applications into enterprise portals by means of portlets is covered in chapter 9. Existing inter-portlet communication mechanisms have limitations as they are not generic enough and do not consider the semantics of the communication. As a solution, a context-based portlet integration approach is proposed in chapter 10.

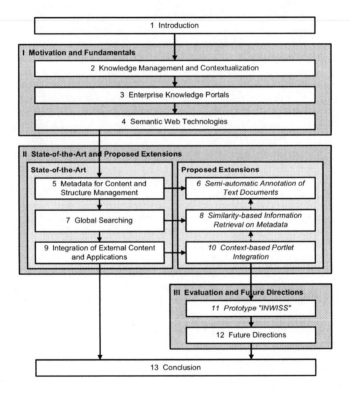

Figure 1.2: Chapter structure

Part III: Evaluation and Future Directions

The INWISS knowledge portal prototype is presented in chapter 11. It is used to evaluate the proposals from part II. Chapter 12 discusses future research directions. Finally, chapter 13 summarizes and concludes this work.

The main scientific contribution of this work is the proposed context-based portlet integration in chapter 10 as it finally allows to combine structured information accessed through application portlets with unstructured information from content management, which is to our knowledge unique. The information retrieval approach from chapter 8 is rather a byproduct of this main proposal, however it is required for a proper evaluation. Also, when dealing with searching on semantic metadata, it is necessary to deal with the creation of such metadata. This is why the semi-automatic approach in chapter 6 is included. These dependencies are depicted by the dashed arrows in figure 1.2.

A box like this at the beginning of each of the remaining chapters will shortly discuss its role for the design research effort presented in this work and particularly comment on its scientific contribution.

Part I

Motivation and Fundamentals

Chapter 2

Knowledge Management and Contextualization

Within the design research effort presented in this work, this chapter has the role of creating the *awareness of the problem* that is being addressed: the unsatisfying integration of structured and unstructured information and its contextualization in enterprises. The motivation, technical requirements, as well as related work are discussed.

In the context of current economical and technological trends such as e-commerce and increased customer orientation, enterprises recognize the necessity to deal with both internal and external knowledge more efficiently and more effectively. Due to a modularization and specialization of enterprises and markets on the one hand and globalization on the other hand the complexity of business processes increases significantly. Furthermore, the amount of existing and potentially relevant information grows, while the response time within these processes continues to decrease. With the rising knowledge-intensity of business processes knowledge is increasingly perceived as a basis for innovation speed, process efficiency, product quality, and the ability to recognize customer potentials; it can have a crucial influence on the competitiveness of enterprises [Bs99, Nur98, DB94].

The name for the fourth success factor, information, has meanwhile been replaced by the term knowledge, the terminology is however not very clearly shaped. The terms data, information, and knowledge are often used as synonyms. Although they are highly connected, they do however not represent equivalent concepts, but can rather be seen as a hierarchical system based

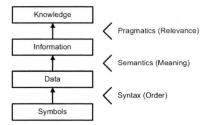

Figure 2.1: Data, information, and knowledge and their semiotic levels [Aug90]

on their semiotic levels as shown in figure 2.1 [Aug90, p. 16]. *Data* consists of an ordered number of different or identical symbols (syntactic level). Combined with a meaning, data forms *information* (semantic level). Usable (i.e. relevant) information that is provided in the right context can be considered as *knowledge* (pragmatic level). Hence, information forms an intermediate stage on the way from data to knowledge; it is "knowledge on the move" [BL02].

> Nonaka & Takehuchi [NT95] define *information* as "a flow of meaningful messages" and *knowledge* as "commitments and beliefs created from these messages".

> Davenport & Prusak [DP98] define *data* as "a set of discrete facts", *information* as "a message meant to change the receiver's perception", and *knowledge* as "a fluid mix of framed experience, values, contextual information, and expert insight that provides a framework for evaluating and incorporating new experience and information. Knowledge originates and is applied in the mind of knowers. In organizations, it often becomes embedded not only in documents or repositories but also in organizational routines, processes, practices, and norms."

> Likewise, Probst et al. [PRR99] define *knowledge* as "the whole of the skills and abilities, which are used by individuals for the solution of problems. Knowledge draws on data and information, which is understood, brought into context, evaluated, compared, linked, and exchanged by humans."

In addition, Nonaka & Takehuchi [NT95] differentiate between implicit and explicit knowledge: *Implicit knowledge* exists in the heads of individuals and is either not yet made explicit or is unreachable by attempts of being made explicit. *Explicit knowledge* exists already in a physical (including electronic) form, namely as information (and data). The transformation of implicit into explicit knowledge is one of the key tasks of knowledge management. On the other hand, according to Maier [Mai04], knowledge comprises observations that have been meaningfully organized and embedded in a context through experience, communication, or inference that an actor uses to interpret situations and to accomplish tasks. Hence, explicit knowledge can also be seen as contextualized information.

Like knowledge, also the term knowledge management is not clearly shaped in the literature. Reasons lie in the complexity of the topic, but also in the different views on it, as a quotation by Karl Sveiby shows [Raj01]: "The term knowledge management has been defined (by management consultants), redefined (by computer scientists), and undefined (by marketers of software products)."

> Maier [Mai04] defines *knowledge management* as "the management function responsible for the regular selection, implemnentation, and evaluation of goal-oriented knowledge strategies that aim at improving an organization's way of handling knowledge internal and external to the organization in order to improve organizational performance. The implementation of knowledge strategies comprises all person-oriented, organizational, and technological instruments suitable to dynamically optimize the organization-wide level of competencies, education, and ability to learn of the members of the organization as well as to develop collective intelligence."

Without stressing the discussion on terminology, the goal of this work is to fullfil a core aim of knowledge management: supplying employees with contextual and situational information of any kind, i.e. providing them with the right information at the right time. This means that the information should be relevant to the user's current working situation (context). As elaborated below in section 2.3, we consider information stored in structured databases (accessible through application systems) as well as unstructured (often textual) documents.

2.1 Goals of Knowledge Management

Generally, the goal of knowledge management can be seen as the publication of knowledge reserves for enterprise-internal purposes, or at least as the creation of a "knowledge map", which provides information about who possesses which knowledge and how it can be made accessible. The employment of knowledge management is supposed to provide the following advantages for the enterprise [DP98]:

- Reduce the effort for searching for information with fast access to internal and external sources

- Avoid duplicate work

- Faster and more efficient decision making through knowledge transfer

As mentioned above, a primary goal of all knowledge management initiatives is to provide employees with the right information at the right time [Ums90]. *Right information* can be understood as relevant to a user's information need and measured by means of the information retrieval metrics recall and precision [BYRN99] (see also in chapter 7). Recall is defined as the amount of relevant information that is retrieved relative to the overall amount of relevant information that exists "out there". Many knowledge management systems (KMS) have concentrated on raising the recall by including information from various different sources. However, with today's information overflow we are often "drowning in information but starving for knowledge" [Nai82]. Hence, precision is defined as the proportion of relevant information among the information that is retrieved, i.e. optimizing the precision means filtering out irrelevant information.

At the right time refers to the fact that the information should be provided situational, i.e. targeted to the user's current information need. Regular KMS are isolated tools that have evolved from the tradition of information management and retrieval. They rely on the user to formulate his/her information need as explicit search queries. In order to provide an efficient and timely information delivery the queries need to be proactive and contextualized [Car03a], i.e. the system should provide a mechanism that automatically delivers information that is relevant the user's current working situation.

From this background we can identify two main requirements that need to be addressed: *integration* and *contextualization*. On the one hand, information from different (structured and unstructured) sources needs to be integrated in order to allow for a global retrieval. On the other hand, the information needs to be put into context and specifically those elements should be provided that the user needs in his/her current context. The main challenges are to define a proper context model, to automatically recognize the user's current context, and to (dynamically) decide which elements are suited best to support users in a certain context [Kle00].

Dey & Abowd [DA99] give a broad definition of context as "any information that can be used to characterize the situation of an entity; an entity is a person, place, or object that is considered relevant to the interaction between a user and an application, including the user and application themselves".

The situation of a person can be described by its user, working, and interaction context [HM03]. Our interpretation of this user model is elaborated in detail in chapter 10. The context of knowledge elements comprises person-related information (e.g., author, target group, expert), related topics, geographical location (e.g., of organizational unit, of creation), type of knowledge (e.g., technical format, conceptual structure), and time (e.g., creation, modification date) [MS02]. Chapter 5 discusses the use of metadata for representing the context of knowledge elements.

In the following we first review (process-oriented) knowledge management literature and show how the theories motivate integration and contextualization as major challenges. Second, we take a look at knowledge management systems and related work that deals with the integration of structured and unstructured information. Finally, we present related work that deals with context-based information retrieval.

2.2 Process-oriented Knowledge Management

Knowledge management (KM) can only be successful if the resource knowledge is professionally managed as a core competency. This has effects on the processes, which identify, generate, organize, and manage knowledge in enterprises. But not only knowledge processes are concerned, but also and in particular the operational business processes which use and develop knowledge for the creation of products and services.

Process-oriented knowledge management suggests to focus on enhancing the efficiency of knowledge work in the context of business processes and by this way link KM efforts to the value chains of organizations, which in accordance to Porter [Por85] particularly contribute to the actual creation of value [EK03, MR03]. On a strategic level, i.e. the analysis and design of processes and knowledge management activities, this leads to combined methods and modeling approaches. On a technical level integration technologies and approaches for process and context-sensitive information delivery are required.

A number of attempts of integrating knowledge management and business processes can be found in the literature. Based on Lehner [Leh00] two different perspectives of process-orientated knowledge management can be differentiated that are discussed in the following.

2.2.1 Managing Knowledge Processes

The first approach focuses on the optimization of processes that are related to the components of knowledge management. Knowledge management activities, e.g., the storage, distribution, and utilization of knowledge, are formulated as processes [FK01]. Knowledge processes and the relations between them, knowledge management activities, and knowledge flows are in the center of consideration. This concept is also concerned with the inner view of knowledge processes, i.e. which generic basic activities they contain and how these can be linked to a value chain. The advantage of regarding knowledge management under a process-orientated angle is the transferability of the various operational measures of process orientation such as process management and controlling on knowledge management activities.

In the context of the knowledge-management-driven approach of integrating process and knowledge management a number of concepts and models have been developed in the literature; the most well-known ones are:

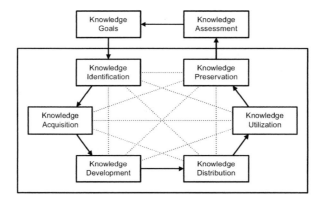

Figure 2.2: Building blocks of knowledge management according to Probst et al. [PRR99]

- Building Blocks of Knowledge Management by Probst et al. [PRR99]

- Improving Knowledge Work Processes by Davenport at al. [DJB96]

- Knowledge Management Practices by Wiig [Wii95, Wii99]

Exemplarily, we will describe the model of Probst et al. [PRR99] in more detail, which offers a practice-oriented approach for implementing knowledge management in an enterprise. It describes the introduction of knowledge management not as linear process model but as the establishment of a continuous improvement process.

The model is probably the most common, practically proven guide for setting up a knowledge management system. It comprises eight components (see figure 2.2), which form a process-oriented model and serve as search rasters for finding problems and deriving suitable starting points for improvement. The components form two knowledge management cycles, an inner and an outer one. The inner cycle is composed of the building blocks of knowledge identification, acquisition, development, distribution, utilization, and preservation:

- *Knowledge identification* is the process where external knowledge for analyzing and describing the organization's knowledge environment is identified.

- *Knowledge acquisition* refers to the forms of expertise the organization should acquire from outside through its relationship with customers, suppliers, competitors and partners.

- *Knowledge development* is a building block which complements knowledge acquisition. Its focus is on generating new skills, new products, better ideas, and more efficient processes. Knowledge development includes all management efforts consciously aiming at producing capabilities.

- *Knowledge distribution* is the process of sharing and spreading knowledge which is already present within the organization.

- *Knowledge utilization* consists of carrying out activities to make sure that the knowledge present in the organization is properly applied.

- *Knowledge preservation* takes care of saving the gained knowledge in form of information, documents, and experiences for future re-use.

There are two additional processes in the outer cycle, knowledge goals and knowledge assessment, which provide the connection to a full knowledge management cycle:

- *Knowledge goals* determine which capabilities should be built on which level.

- *Knowledge assessment* completes the cycle, providing the essential data for strategic control of knowledge management.

Each component is assigned to a set of intervention quadrants, i.e. influence factors that need to be shaped individually for the respective project or enterprise. In the context of this approach, process-oriented knowledge management is seen as the optimization of the individual processes or components of knowledge management.

2.2.2 Supporting Business Processes with Knowledge Management

The second approach covers process management activities, which are aligned to knowledge-intensive business processes and the use of knowledge management instruments. In contrast to the first approach, which emanates predominantly from knowledge management and introduces specific knowledge processes, this approach pursues the goal of supplementing already existing operational processes with knowledge management activities. Hence, this concept sees process-oriented knowledge management as an approach for a more or less radical improvement of processes in the sense of business process reengineering (BPR). It leads to an iterative adjustment of knowledge-intensive business processes and can thus also be described as knowledge-oriented process management. Business processes are seen both as triggers and drivers of knowledge management [Hei01, Bs99]. Knowledge creation and utilization happens within business processes, which provide the context in which the information is embedded.

Böhm & Härtwig [BH05] present an approach for a demand-meeting and contextualized information supply within business processes in enterprises. With the orientation at value-creating business processes the approach aims at integrating a knowledge management solution into the already existing, process-executing systems. The users are supported in an individual, task-oriented fashion by deriving role and task contexts from the business process model. The goal is to avoid that the use of knowledge management systems, which are usually perceived by employees as additional information sources, creates additional work rather than facilitation. KMS should be integrated into the daily work routine of the users as transparently as possible.

For this purpose the idea of a Pre-Built Information Space (PreBIS) was developed. An information space is the amount of information, which results from the context of a certain task or role situation and is needed in order to satisfy the information need in this situational context. Within the space information is weighted concerning its relevance in the current context and presented selectively in order to avoid swamping the user with too much (insignificant) information.

The implementation of this approach leads to a context-based information retrieval system, which together with other similar approaches is covered below in section 2.4.

2.3 Knowledge Management Systems

The first wave of knowledge management (or rather data and information management) has concentrated on structured information that is stored in databases and made accessible through

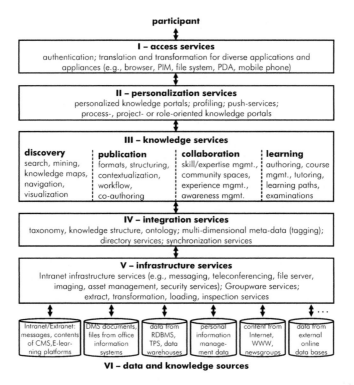

participant

I – access services
authentication; translation and transformation for diverse applications and appliances (e.g., browser, PIM, file system, PDA, mobile phone)

II – personalization services
personalized knowledge portals; profiling; push-services;
process-, project- or role-oriented knowledge portals

III – knowledge services

discovery	publication	collaboration	learning
search, mining, knowledge maps, navigation, visualization	formats, structuring, contextualization, workflow, co-authoring	skill/expertise mgmt., community spaces, experience mgmt., awareness mgmt.	authoring, course mgmt., tutoring, learning paths, examinations

IV – integration services
taxonomy, knowledge structure, ontology; multi-dimensional meta-data (tagging);
directory services; synchronization services

V – infrastructure services
Intranet infrastructure services (e.g., messaging, teleconferencing, file server, imaging, asset management, security services); Groupware services; extract, transformation, loading, inspection services

Intranet/Extranet: messages, contents of CMS,E-learning platforms	DMS documents, files from office information systems	data from RDBMS, TPS, data warehouses	personal information management data	content from Internet, WWW, newsgroups	data from external online data bases

VI – data and knowledge sources

Figure 2.3: Architecture of a knowledge management system [Mai04]

application systems [Leh00]. The term business intelligence has been framed for a set of tools that make this structured information available in an efficient manner. In particular, OLAP (Online Analytical Processing) reporting techniques [CD97] use multidimensional data models to provide intuitive query interfaces for end users.

Large amounts of the information in today's enterprises – according to a study by Goldman Sachs 80-90% – exist however as unstructured documents rather than structured database data. In addition, another study by IDC showed that in large organizations the number of documents doubles every two months [Fel01]. As a consequence, a second wave has addressed the management of such unstructured documents by introducing document management systems (DMS) that provide a central repository and optimized search features. In a third wave, these systems have then been enhanced with additional (particularly collaboration) functionality and are now known as knowledge management systems (KMS) [Mai04].

For a long time, the areas of structured and unstructured information have been rather isolated, although knowledge management vendors have very well recognized the need for integration. There were a number of efforts (in research and industry) to couple business intelligence with knowledge (or document) management. Authors like Maier [Mai04] propose architectures that include structured as well as unstructured data sources (e.g., figure 2.3). However there are usually no (technical) details given how "true" integration can be achieved.

Integration means more than just global searching. The goal is that users can access the information from one single user interface. For this purpose portal technology has converged with knowledge management systems, forming a new generation of systems called enterprise knowledge portals (see chapter 3). Portals allow integrating different applications on a user interface level by combining different webpage fragments on a single portal page. This technology can be used for accessing unstructured data (document and content management) and structured data (business intelligence and operational applications) through the same user interface.

Rieger et al. [RKvM00] address the integration of unstructured (or semi-structured) documents with structured OLAP data. They treat OLAP cubes as "documents" stored in a digital library like repository and use manually created metadata to link them to related documents. These manual links are obviously problematic. The ontology-based approach presented in this work uses metadata that can be automatically derived from OLAP report definitions (or any other semantic representation of a resource). This approach is to some respect similar to the one presented by Audersch [Aud02], however their approach only works for their individual OLAP system.

In addition, the navigation within the structured data has so far been untouched by the integration. Both Rieger et al. [RKvM00] and Audersch [Aud02] treat OLAP cubes or reports as monolithic elements. Ad-hoc navigation is not considered, i.e. it is not possible to navigate by means of OLAP operations (slicing/dicing, drill-down/roll-up) and use the resulting query context to search for related documents. Generalizing this deficiency to other (non-OLAP) applications leads again to the above requirement of contextualization and context-based information retrieval.

2.4   Context-based Information Retrieval

The PreBIS approach [BH05] mentioned above in section 2.2.2 provides a situated, context-based information delivery. A so-called contextualized information system is attuned to an organization in a pre-build phase, i.e. it is concretely modeled for a specific use. The modeled context consists of static (modeled roles, tasks, and information needs), dynamic (changeable by the user, e.g., search terms and strategies), and organizational (personal qualifications and experiences, location, technical environment) elements. This is also the limitation of the approach, as a short-term context that evolves from an interaction with (operational or analytical) application systems is not considered.

The KnowMore project [ABM+00, Mau01] proposes the use of context information that can be derived from a workflow management system, in order to supply users with context-sensitive information that is relevant to their current task. For this purpose information on the current task context is taken from the workflow and organizational model and transferred into a query on a document base. The result of this query is a number of documents, which are to support the user of the workflow system in fulfilling his/her current task. The DECOR (Delivery of Context-sensitive Organisational Knowledge) project [ABN+01] tries to extend the ideas from the KnowMore project, that were originally developed for strongly structured processes, to weakly structured processes. Classical modeling methods for business processes are extended by specific knowledge management functions and supported in the modeling phase by specific tools such as the K-Modeler. The result is however no executable business process, but a model, which is rather suitable for analytic purposes.

A further approach, which uses business processes as a context-giving system, emanates from the POKER (Process Oriented Knowledge Delivery) project [Fen02]. It aims in particular at weakly structured processes, which are often executed with standard office applications (word processing, spreadsheet). It emphasizes the automatic recognition of process segments (template matching) and the observation of the user application (client-side monitoring). Similarly, the Lumiere project [HBH+98] provides a wizard for users of an office application. A user model permits the identification of latent information needs on the basis of user actions within the application system. From these latent information needs the system derives supplementary texts and offers them to the user.

The Remembrance Agent [Rho00] reads the text of a document, which a user currently works with, in order to look continuously for similar documents. A characteristic of this kind of context-considering retrieval is the non-obtrusive kind of presenting the results to the user, which takes place in its own window or part of the screen. Beside purely textual content Watson [BH00] observes also the type of application used, for example whether it is a word processing application, an email client, or a web browser, and evaluates available metadata, e.g., the document author. Watson uses a set of Internet search engines for retrieving relevant information.

Both Letizia [Lie97] and WebWatcher [JFM97] are examples of systems, which aim at supporting a user with his/her navigation on the Internet by suggesting other interesting or similar pages. As a basis they use the currently viewed page in the web browser as well as interest profiles. Letizia observes the surf behavior of each individual user in order to conclude their interests. It finds similar or potentially interesting pages by recursively following hyperlinks from the currently viewed page to other pages. WebWatcher also supervises the surf behavior of the users. Contrary to Letizia it uses reinforcement learning[1] together with the hyperlinks and the Vector Space Model (see also chapter 7) for developing the user model.

Context-based information retrieval has also been studied by Henrich & Morgenroth [HM02] who propose a high-level architecture for finding documents relevant to the context of the user. They propose to include plug-ins in client applications that would communicate the user's interaction context to an information retrieval engine. However, most application programs will not easily allow the integration of plug-ins. For this reason and due to the difficulty of identifying and translating a user context to an IR query in a totally generic way, the authors have concentrated on the particular use within the software development environment in more recent publications [HM03].

If combined with a fuzzy metadata-based retrieval approach as presented in chapter 8 the context-based portlet integration proposed in chapter 10 provides implicit "find related" searches based on the current user context. However, context-based information retrieval is only one application of the rather general approach. In another scenario, a sales application target portlet might, for example, use the received context as default values for creating a new quote, or a content management portlet might use it as default metadata for a new document.

---
[1]*Reinforcement learning* is a machine learning approach that learns behavior in a dynamic environment through trial-and-error interactions [KLM96].

Chapter 3

Enterprise Knowledge Portals

Portals are more and more seen as a "standard workplace" for employees due to their ability to combine different applications and information sources on a single web-based user interface. With the convergence of portal and knowledge management functionality, enterprise knowledge portals are the solution of choice for providing an integrated access to structured and unstructured information. Within the design research effort presented in this work, this chapter gives an overview on enterprise knowledge portals and identifies remaining open issues (*awareness of problem phase*) that are then addressed in part II (*suggestion phase*).

The term portal is frequently used in information technology. However, there is a variety of definitions and no clear demarcation. The term has its origin in ancient architecture; it is derived from the Latin word "porta", which means something like door or gate and designates a monumentally shaped entrance of a building. In an IT context the term portal has evolved as a designation for an entrance website on the Internet.

While in the early days the Internet was only used by a handful of experts, the number of users (and available sites) has quickly exploded. First attempts to structure and bundle the offered information appeared as link collections. These were enhanced with search functionality and a categorization of the information, providing a central entry point to the World Wide Web. This first generation of portals was further extended with personalization features making it possible to arrange information according to a user's individual needs and desires. The benefits of portals were soon also discovered by enterprises. Intranets were extended by the functionality that was already successful on the Internet; the first enterprise portals were created.

Davydov [Dav01] defines a portal as "a doorway to the cyber world of information. It is not a product sold by a vendor, but a goal to be achieved through the integration of multiple products from multiple vendors. It is a concept of a unification platform that allows for a collection of application services to work together to facilitate access to that world of information. The ability to aggregate these services and to provide the necessary platform for them to work cooperatively are the real values of this concept, in general, and of corporate portals, in particular."

Likewise, Larry Bowden [Bow], IBM Vice President of Portal Solutions, defines a portal as "a single integrated point of comprehensive, ubiquitous, and useful access to information, applications, and people" .

A more technical definition is given in the recent Java Portlet Specification [JCP04]: "A portal is a web-based application that – commonly – provides personalization, single-sign-on, content aggregation from different sources and hosts on the presentation layer of information systems. Aggregation is the action of integrating content from different sources within a webpage. A portal may have sophisticated personalization features to provide customized content to users. Portal pages may have different sets of portlets creating content for different users."

From this background the main characteristics of portals can be easily identified: They serve as an entry point for the information offered on the Internet or an intranet. Portals structure this information, offer search capabilities, and provide means for personalization. We will elaborate these characteristics in more detail in the following subsections. So far users depended on switching between different separate applications for performing their daily activities. Portals bundle these applications and provide a uniform presentation layer. As the last of the above definitions already reveals, so-called "portlets" are used for integrating content and applications into portals. This concept will be covered below in section 3.3.

3.1   Classification of Portals

As mentioned above portals have been deployed in different environments. Hence different types of portals can be distinguished. Different classification schemes have been used in the literature. A first classification criterion is the degree of specialization [TKL+03], i.e. the broadness of the topics attainable through the portal. We distinguish between horizontal and vertical portals:

- A *horizontal portal* covers a variety of topic areas and puts no focus on a certain target group or a certain topic. An example of a horizontal portal is Yahoo![1], which provides a wide range of information on many different topics (news, finance, sports, travel, etc.).

- *Vertical portals* address specific topics (e.g., lines of business or product areas), which are however covered in more detail. An example of a vertical portal is a travel portal specialized in vacation trips. Apart from providing information about possible destinations, services for booking journeys, suitable insurances, etc. may also be offered.

Similarly, based on Gurzki et al. [GHE02], we distinguish between web and business portals:

- *Web portals* are (usually horizontal) portals that provide an entry point to the World Wide Web, offering broad and editorially managed information together with selected link lists. A good example is again Yahoo! (see above). The main characteristic of web portals is their openness, i.e. they are accessible for everyone.

- *Business portals* on the other hand usually target a closed user group that has particular interest in a certain business. Apart from a usually vertically aligned information offer on special topics, business portals provide also a number of services around these topics.

Business portals can be further subdivided by the type of users that they address [SW02]. Despite the long-term goal of operating only one central portal with many role-specific occurrences (through personalization), the portal architecture of many enterprises is rather scattered. We differentiate between consumer or B2C (business-to-consumer), partner or B2B (business-to-business), and enterprise or B2E (business-to-employee) portals:

---

[1]http://www.yahoo.com

- *Consumer or B2C portals* address different customer segments. Product information and specific services are offered. For example, an online shop can be integrated into the portal.

- *Partner or B2B portals* serve the information sharing and transaction processing among enterprises, e.g., suppliers, development partners, etc. Hence, they are often also called supplier portals. Security considerations, i.e. providing only authorized users with portal access, play a particular role.

- *Enterprise or B2E portals* are usually the core of intranets. They provide the employees of an enterprise with the information and applications they need to fulfill their individual business tasks. This requires an elaborated role model as a basis for personalized portal views.

Finally, three types of enterprise portals can be distinguished based on the functionality they provide. We distinguish between enterprise information, application, and knowledge portals:

- *Enterprise information portals* are used to publish (usually unstructured) information. They offer functionality for structuring, authoring, and search, just like regular intranets based on content management systems. By adding personalization features they constitute themselves as portals.

- *Enterprise application portals* provide access to operational (e.g., ERP) and business intelligence application systems. In addition to unstructured information also structured information (stored in databases) can be accessed, usually by integrating application portlets into the portal user interface.

- *Enterprise knowledge portals* offer the possibility to collect and manage knowledge and to transfer it among employees. The term is often used as a synonym for enterprise information portals. However, the focus is more on user-driven knowledge management rather than centrally published content. In addition, collaboration features like bulletin boards are offered.

In practice a typical enterprise portal contains elements from all of these types. Newer developments also try to incorporate workflow functionality to control the page and application flow, constituting the term "process portal". Business processes are usually supported only in fragments by different application systems. Portals provide the potential to integrate these applications along the line of the business processes without the need of changing the applications that support the subprocesses.

3.2 Reference Architecture

The portal products offered on the market differ substantially (see section 3.4), they usually only provide part of the mentioned functionality. Nevertheless, Gurzki & Hinderer [GH03] identify fundamental similarities in the architectures of enterprise portals. A reference architecture based on their findings is shown in figure 3.1.

The architecture follows the classical 3-tier paradigm with presentation, application, and data layer. The client devices that visualize the portal pages, usually a web browser, are found on the presentation layer. The application layer represents the core of the portal system. For many vendors the portal is dependent on an application server or part of a platform solution (e.g., J2EE or .NET) which contains an application server. *Delivery services* are responsible

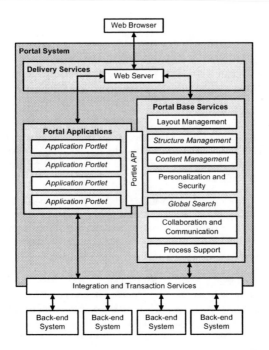

Figure 3.1: Portal reference architecture (based on [GH03])

for delivering the portal pages to the presentation layer. Portal applications are represented by so-called *application portlets* as elaborated in the next section. Within the portal system, the application portlets are accessed via a software interface (portlet API), through which the portlets can also utilize the portal base services. These base services provide the core functionality that constitutes enterprise (knowledge) portals:

- *Layout management* is responsible for rendering and combining the portal webpage before it is presented to the client device.

- *Structure management* defines the structure within the portal. This involves particularly the navigation between the different portal applications, but also within the portal content managed by the content management base service (see below). The integration of portal and content navigation is a crucial (and non-trivial) issue, especially if an external content management system is used.

- The *content management* service subsumes content, document and knowledege management functions. It serves the collection and structuring of knowledge, and thus the efficient organization of the knowledge transfer between employees [Col03, pp. 49ff]. External content and document management systems can be integrated for this purpose. They support authoring and administration of portal content (i.e. portal articles as well as other documents). Content management is highly interwoven with search functionality (see below), which is required for regaining the information stored in the documents.

- *Personalization and security* features deal with the creation and management of user accounts and provide a single-sign-on for the portal applications. A role concept provides individual portal views (personalized in terms of content, design, and layout). Personalization is often regarded as one of the most substantial concepts of a portal. For this purpose, the users need to be registered and authenticated whenever they visit the portal. In many cases an (enterprise-wide) directory service is available. The portal can use this directory service for user registration and authentication, e.g., through the LDAP (Lightweight Directory Access Protocol) standard.

- *Global search* functionality provides searches across the data sources that are incorporated into the portal, e.g., content and document management systems, databases, corporate applications, external sources (e.g., the Internet). Since portals provide access to a vast amount of information, comfortable and flexible search functions are inevitable for making this information usable.

- *Collaboration and communication* features include email, group calendars, discussion groups, etc., often realized by integrating an existing email or groupware system.

- *Process support* is achieved by integrating workflow functionality into the portal in order to automate the page flow and guide the user from application to application.

On the back-end, operational (e.g., ERP) or analytical (e.g., business intelligence) application systems or data sources like relational databases or external content management systems can be found. Integration and transaction services provide the interfaces to those back-end systems and arrange for distributed transaction security. The functionality ranges from simple database interfaces (e.g., JDBC, ODBC) over classic application middleware to sophisticated enterprise application integration (EAI) solutions. For some vendors the integration and transaction services are part of the application server platform rather than the portal.

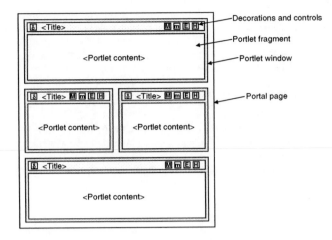

Figure 3.2: Elements of a portal page [JCP04]

As elaborated in chapter 2, the main focus of this work is on providing an integrated access to structured and unstructured information. With regard to the reference architecture, unstructured documents are managed by the *content management* portal base service. The navigation among those documents is addressed by the *structure management*, finding documents (and resources from other sources) by a *global search* facility. Structured information is stored in databases and made accessible through application systems represented by *application portlets*. Hence, these areas (shown itallic in figure 3.1) are covered in more detail in part II.

3.3 Portlets

A main characteristic of a portal is the possibility to integrate applications by representing them uniformly within a single portal user interface. Portals serve as a central point of access to all applications needed for a certain business task, eliminating the need for users to switch between different applications.

As already mentioned above, the applications are represented by so-called portlets[2] [Weg02, MS04]. Each portlet controls a rectangular part of the portal webpage. Portlets deliver content (usually HTML) fragments that are, together with the portal frame and portlet decorations, combined by the portal software. Figure 3.2 shows a schematic view of a portal page with four portlets [JCP04].

From a user's point of view a portlet represents a visual information or application unit on the portal page. By means of portlets webpages, applications, and information channels of news providers can be accessed. Thus portlets integrate business-process-specific functionality and offer a homogeneous entry point to different information sources and different, independent

---

[2]In the literature the term portlet has become widely accepted. It is used by most portal vendors (IBM, SUN, BEA, Oracle, etc.), however, also other terms have appeared for the same thing, e.g., iView (SAP), Gadget (Plumtree), or Web Part (Microsoft) [MS04].

applications. The functionality of portlets can range from, e.g., reading and sending emails, querying a search engine, accessing stock quotes, and viewing intranet articles, up to accessing a bill of material in an ERP or a sales report in a business intelligence application. Portlets play an important role for personalization [TKL+03]. Users can subscribe to certain portlets, i.e. they can select the relevant ones from the available set, provided that the required permissions exist.

From a technical point of view portlets are reusable software components, similar to servlets [JCP03], only that they provide portal-specific functionality and are not rendered standalone but being integrated into a portal page. Like servlets they are made accessible via a web browser. Most portal systems provide a number of portlets for integrated functionality (e.g., content management) out-of-the-box, generic portlets for the integration of external content and applications, as well as the possibility to develop specialized portlets for specific back-end applications; details will be discussed in chapter 9. Portlets are based on an interface definition by the portal vendor (the portal or portlet API). A recently standardized interface for portlet development in a Java environment is the Java Portlet Specification (also known as JSR 168) [JCP04]. In addition, a standard for accessing portlets remotely via web services called WSRP (Web Services for Remote Portlets) [OAS03] is available. Details on the Java Portlet Specification and WSRP follow in section 9.3.

Portals offer the possibility to bundle and uniformly present heterogeneous applications. A problem however persists with exchanging data between those applications. Data values often have to be copied manually from one portlet to the other. In order to provide a user-oriented integration, inter-portlet communication means are required that allow the automated data exchange between two or more portlets. Links between portlets and corresponding behavior can be achieved. For example, the selection of an employee in a portlet can automatically trigger viewing his/her personnel data in a human resources portlet, or the supplier address that is viewed in one portlet can be used in another portlet for the creation of an order [Dav01, p. 18].

Inter-portlet communication operates on a front-end (user interface) level. The back-end systems are untouched, i.e. no back-end integration is performed. In order to create a flexible integrative architecture, it is thus desirable to combine inter-portlet communication and enterprise application integration (EAI). This trend is also reflected on the market, where EAI and portal solutions start to converge [SW02].

Some of today's portal systems provide certain features for portlet messaging, e.g., the SAP Enterprise Portal Client Framework and IBM's Click-to-Action and Cooperative Portlets (see below). However, these are so far proprietary; portlet standards such as the Java Portlet Specification (JSR 168) and WSRP define no inter-portlet communication features (see chapter 9). In addition, the existing approaches require extensive custom programming and are unsuitable for coupling portlets that are provided as third-party software components. Chapter 10 presents a novel generic, context-based approach for portlet integration using Semantic Web technologies.

3.4 Selected Portal Solutions

At present numerous portal solutions exist on the market, which follow the above reference architecture to different degrees. The range of the portal functionality offered by an individual portal vendor usually depends on its origin. Therefore we can roughly divide the portal industry into the following four classes (adapted from [MS04, p. 45]):

- Application infrastructure and middleware vendors

- Business software and ERP system vendors

- Portal specialists

- Vendors of content and document management systems

Among the application infrastructure and middleware vendors that regard their portal product as an addition to their platform strategy are, for example, IBM, Microsoft, and BEA. The business software vendors SAP, Oracle, and Siebel offer a portal solution, which particularly aims at integrating their own applications. Plumtree and Viador are pure portal specialists; they have shaped the term enterprise portal and can be regarded as independent technology vendors. Examples for vendors of content and document management systems are Vignette and Interwoven. Beside those commercial vendors there are also some open source portal solutions such as Apache Jetspeed[3], Jahia[4], and uPortal[5].

We present five selected portal solutions in more detail: The commercial solutions by IBM, SAP, Microsoft, and Plumtree are covered, as they have a particularly important position on the portal market [MS04, p. 45]. In addition we give an overview on Apache Jetspeed, which has no notable market share, however, as an open source system serves as a basis for our prototype implementation (see chapter 11). In accordance to the research goal of this work, the portal solutions will be analyzed particularly for their capabilities for content management, global searching, and application integration and portlet development. Special attention will be paid to inter-portlet communication and the support of the portlet standards JSR 168 (Java Portlet Specification) and WSRP. For details on these standards see chapter 9.

3.4.1   Apache Jetspeed

Apache Jetspeed[6], currently available in release 1.5, is a platform independent (Java and XML-based) open source portal framework, which is developed within the Portals project of the Apache Software Foundation (ASF). The architecture of Jetspeed is based on a number of other open source components such as Apache Turbine[7] and Torque[8].

Jetspeed provides a number of generic portlets, such as the HTML Portlet for viewing static HTML pages that are stored on the portal server, the Webpage Portlet for integrating external web-based applications, the RSS Portlet for content syndication based on RSS[9], as well as portlets for the administration of the portal. The Jetspeed Content Portlet provides a basic content management system, which is however still rather limited; the integration of other systems is possible and should be preferred [TKL+03, pp. 256ff]. Likewise, there is no reasonable global search engine included out-of-the-box. By means of a programming interface (portlet API) new portlets can be developed in Java. Jetspeed currently provides no standardized functions for realizing inter-portlet communication, some kind of portlet messaging can however be achieved with some adjustments [TKL+03, pp. 240ff]. The implementation of our INWISS portal prototype[10] is based on Apache Jetspeed; technical details follow in chapter 11.

---

[3]http://portals.apache.org/jetspeed-1/
[4]http://www.jahia.org
[5]http://www.uportal.org
[6]http://portals.apache.org/jetspeed-1/
[7]http://jakarta.apache.org/turbine/
[8]http://db.apache.org/torque/
[9]RSS is an XML-based exchange format for content. Depending on the version, RSS stands for "RDF Site Summary", "Really Simple Syndication", or "Rich Site Summary"; for details see chapter 9.
[10]http://www.inwiss.org

Jetspeed 1 (i.e. up to release 1.5) offers neither support for the Java Portlet Specification (JSR 168) nor for the WSRP portlet standard. However, a redesign called Jetspeed 2 is currently under development. It is based on Apache Pluto[11], the reference implementation of the Java Portlet Specification and, in addition to supporting the standard, offers a more scalable component-based architecture.

3.4.2 IBM WebSphere Portal Server

IBM WebSphere is a software infrastructure that evolved from a pure application server to a complete product family with a common basis. The IBM WebSphere Portal Server[12] (currently in release 5.1) is a J2EE application executed on the IBM WebSphere Application Server and provides a framework for implementing enterprise portals. The WebSphere Portal Server is partly based on the Apache Jetspeed portal solution (see above), however, the two differ in many concepts, e.g., in the way portlets are implemented [TKL+03, p. 227].

The IBM WebSphere Portal Server offers comprehensive functionality for providing access to content, applications and business processes to portal users. The users need to login only once into the portal (single-sign-on) and are then authenticated via an LDAP directory for every integrated application. IBM integrates the document and content management system DB2 Content Manager and provides enterprise search functions in its "Extend" version of the portal.

IBM provides a portlet container, which allows integrating arbitrary applications based on standards like J2EE, web services, and XML. Portlets can be developed by using the programming interface of the portal server (portlet API), which is very similar to the Java Portlet Specification. The WebSphere Portal Toolkit provides templates and a development and test environment for portlets. In addition, the so-called Portlet Builder permits a point-and-click portlet development without Java programming. As a mechanism for inter-portlet communication IBM provides the Click-to-Action (C2A) technology and the concept of Cooperative Portlets [RC03]. Details on this technology follow as related work in section 10.1.

WebSphere contains a limited number of generic portlets in its portlet catalog, which allow the immediate integration of various IBM as well as third party applications. Portlets for email systems (e.g., Lotus Notes and Microsoft Exchange) and a number of other standard applications (e.g., Microsoft Office) are provided [WDB02]. Moreover, IBM offers IFRAME and web clipping technology for the integration of existing websites, as well as RSS for content syndication (see chapter 9).

The IBM WebSphere Portal Server contains a portlet runtime, which permits running portlets that have been developed based on the Java Portlet Specification (JSR 168) [IBM]. The standardized API is however still accompanied by the proprietary IBM portlet API as it contains additional features (e.g., for inter-portlet communication, see above). IBM, one of the initial members of the WSRP standardization committee, supports the WSRP standard both as a producer and as a consumer. The support of WSRP within WebSphere is based on JSR 168, i.e. the WSRP consumer client is implemented as JSR 168 portlet (again, see chapter 9 for details).

3.4.3 SAP Enterprise Portal

The SAP Enterprise Portal[13] (currently in release 6.0), which is based on the SAP NetWeaver technology platform[14], offers personalized access to information and applications to employees,

---

[11]http://portals.apache.org/pluto/

[12]http://www-306.ibm.com/software/genservers/portal/

[13]http://www.sap.com/solutions/netweaver/enterpriseportal/

[14]Since NetWeaver '04 the Enterprise Portal is an integral part of the platform rather than a separate product.

customers, and partners of an enterprise. SAP provides a J2EE-based portal infrastructure with a wide range of functionality. The focus is particularly on application integration, knowledge management, and collaboration [GR04, p. 161].

The core of the SAP Enterprise Portal consists of a number of components: the Page Builder, the Portal Content Directory, the Knowledge Management Platform, the Unification Server, as well as components for user management and security. The Knowledge Management (KM) Platform contains a content management component with advanced features for document categorization as well as a global search engine called TREX. External information sources can be integrated by means of so-called Repository Managers; details follow in section 7.3.

The "portlets" within the SAP Enterprise Portal are called iViews (Integrated Views). iViews are personalizable software components, which represent information and application functionality within the portal. The iView Server makes the iViews available to the client browser and allows them to access portal services, which provide access to back-end systems via connectors (e.g., the SAP Java Connector), user management via LDAP directories, etc. [GR04, pp. 161, 174ff] iViews can be developed in various programming languages, to a large extent iViews are however written in Java (Java iViews) and run by the Java iView Runtime accordingly. Besides, there are iViews, which are based on Microsoft's .NET technology and run by the .NET iView Runtime [GR04, p. 173]. Apart from support for Java and .NET-based iViews, SAP also supports iViews based on web services that are made accessible via UDDI and WSDL and communicate with the iView Server via SOAP [Pop02]. SAP provides an Enterprise Portal Client Framework (EPCF) for client-side communication between iViews [SAP02]. The EPCF is based on JavaScript and Java applets, details follow as related work in section 10.1.

Using iViews SAP applications (SAP R/2 and SAP R/3), the entire SAP NetWeaver Suite, mySAP Business Suite components (e.g., SAP SRM, SAP CRM, or SAP BW), third party applications (Siebel, Baan, PeopleSoft, Oracle, etc.), documents, databases, collaboration tools, legacy systems, internal as well as external web content, web services, and Yahoo! services can be integrated into the portal. SAP provides pre-defined iViews as so-called Business Packages that allow an immediate integration into the SAP Enterprise Portal. Web clipping technology for integrating fragments from (external) websites is provided by means of the iView Catcher and URL iViews [GR04, pp. 164ff, 171ff].

Besides iViews SAP offers a further interesting technology called Unification for accessing structured databases. The access to the different heterogeneous information sources through the Unification Server is based on a Unified Object Model as an abstraction layer. Unification and Drag&Relate provide a navigation mechanism which accesses structured data, analyzes it, and relates it with other structured data [Pop02]. Unfortunately, there is no integration with unstructured data from the KM component (see above). Also Drag&Relate is covered in more detail as related work in section 10.1.

A support for the portlet standards JSR 168 (Java Portlet Specification) and WSRP is so far missing in the SAP Enterprise Portal. Both standards are however planned for NetWeaver '05. The SAP development environment will permit the integration of JSR-168-compatible portlets from other vendors. SAP however still prefers its own iView technology over the JSR 168 standard and will continue to support both APIs. In addition, the SAP Enterprise Portal will support both WSRP consumers and producers. Therefore a simple integration of WSRP-compatible content will be possible and iViews will be publishable as WSRP services.

3.4.4 Microsoft SharePoint Portal Server

The Microsoft SharePoint Portal Server 2003[15] is an enterprise portal platform, which builds upon the Windows SharePoint Services (part of the Windows 2003 Server operating system) and makes a uniform website with personalized content and services available to an entire enterprise, individual departments, or other specific target groups (e.g., partners) [Dow03].

The SharePoint Services are based on the .NET component concept and support team-oriented collaboration and sharing of web content. They allow a simple composition of web-sites, which can contain documents, calendars, contact folders, etc. The SharePoint Portal Server allows the aggregation of these websites on a web portal and adds functionality such as document management, fulltext indexing, and advanced searching [Dow03, WG04, pp. 5ff]. An integrated user and permission management regulates the access rights of the individual users [WG04, pp. 303ff].

The information shown on the SharePoint portal page is represented by so-called Web Parts, Microsoft's counterpart to portlets. Web Parts are closed modules for the integration of infor-mation and applications [Gur03, pp. 92ff]. Technically, they are .NET assemblies, developed in C#, C++ or Visual Basic .NET, that provide HTML fragments [CM04]. The SharePoint in-frastructure also provides support for communication between Web Parts based on standardized interfaces. Users can link Web Parts by means of menu selections. Additionally, transformers are provided, which permit communication between Web Parts, whose interfaces are not ac-curately matching. If a discrepancy is determined, a dialogue box allows the user to transfer values from one interface to another [Bar03].

Microsoft provides a Web Part Gallery, which contains Web Parts for accessing Microsoft applications and products by SAP, Siebel and PeopleSoft [Gur03, p. 92]. Web Parts are provided for business intelligence, CRM, ERP, syndicated content, knowledge management, collabora-tion, project management, etc. An entire website or part of a website (web clipping) can be in-tegrated into a SharePoint portal by means of the Web Capture Web Part [Dow03]. In addition, FrontPage 2003 allows accessing database tables and representing the retrieved information as a Web Part [WG04, p. 365]. By using the SAP .NET Connectors for Visual Studio .NET data from SAP can be presented as a Web Part. The connectors permit the communication between the .NET platform and the SAP system via remote function calls. Furthermore Microsoft offers a SAP-specific Web Part Toolkit. This toolkit provides Web Parts, which make SAP NetWeaver iViews available within the SharePoint Portal Server [Eri04].

The Java Portlet Specification (JSR 168) is not supported by Microsoft, since it is a pure Java specification. Microsoft is member of the WSRP committee and offers a WSRP Web Part Toolkit as well as a WSRP Web Services Toolkit, which allow the integration of applications via web service standards [CM04, p. 20]. The WSRP Web Part Toolkit provides different, standardized integration techniques, including the XML Data View Web Part, and contains a ready-to-install WSRP consumer component for integrating WSRP portlet services into the SharePoint Portal Server. In future, the WSRP Web Services Toolkit will also make the content of a SharePoint page available via WSRP services (as a WSRP producer).

3.4.5 Plumtree Corporate Portal

The Plumtree Enterprise Web Suite[16] with the Plumtree Corporate Portal (currently in release 5.0) offers a general framework for the creation and administration of web applications and con-sists of integration solutions for aggregating resources, base services like collaboration, content

---

[15]http://office.microsoft.com/sharepoint/
[16]http://www.plumtree.com/products/

management and intelligent search, and a portal platform, with which the web applications are presented to a broad target group. It is available both in a Java and a .NET version [KM04, p. 12].

Plumtree is based on a distributable and scalable Web Service Architecture (WSA). Due to this architecture Plumtree portlets do not have to run on the same application server as the portal; they operate as server-side remote services [Mac04]. In addition, Plumtree uses web services also for other portal functions, e.g., indexing content, importing security information, and creating user profiles. The core element of the Plumtree architecture is the Parallel Portal Engine. It offers a WSDL interface for the communication with portlet web services, the Collaboration Server, the Content Server and the Studio Server. These integration components, which can run on separate application servers, communicate with the portal server via HTTP and SOAP [Kel04, pp. 3ff].

Plumtree uses portlets, which were formerly known as Gadget Web Services (or shortly Gadgets), as the main concept for the integration of external data and applications into the portal. Portlets are interactive web components which are executable as remote services on many application servers. The Enterprise Web Development Kit (EDK) offers software, documentation, and code examples for Java and .NET development environments. The .NET version of the EDK supports Visual Basic .NET and C# [Kel04, p. 7]. With the help of the user interface tools in the EDK, Plumtree supports the development of portlets that realize some kind of inter-portlet communication. For this purpose the Portlet Communication Component (PCC) technology allows portlets to communicate via events and to exchange messages.

Plumtree offers a number of portlets for software products by other vendors such as Microsoft, Lotus, SAP, PeopleSoft, Siebel, Interwoven, and Documentum, out-of-the-box. Likewise, Plumtree Integration Frameworks allow the automatic generation of customized portlets for SAP R/3, Siebel, and PeopleSoft [KM04, p. 6]. The Plumtree Content Server, Collaboration Server, and Studio Server provide additional portlets and services for the portal. For example, a pre-built portlet for the integration of websites (web clipping) is managed by the Content Server. In addition, Plumtree offers an RSS-compatible portlet for content syndication (see chapter 9).

Plumtree is one of the first portal vendors, who realize the implementation of both portlet standards, the Java Portlet Specification (JSR 168) and WSRP. The portal communicates with a container, which contains the actual JSR 168 portlet via HTTP. It is therefore not necessary that JSR 168 portlets run on the same platform as the portal, i.e. they can also be integrated into a portal running on .NET. The Plumtree WSRP portlet consumer allows merging WSRP portlets into the Plumtree portal. It serves as a mediator between the portal and the actual WSRP portlet, the so-called WSRP producer. The portal, the WSRP portlet consumer and the portlet producer communicate via HTTP and SOAP and can hence also run on different platforms [Kel03].

The goal of the above survey was to give a short overview of current enterprise portal solutions. We cover individual distinctive features as related work in part II; remaining deficiencies are identified and proposed extensions based on Semantic Web technologies are presented.

We discuss the role of metadata for *content and structure management* in chapter 5 and present a semi-automatic approach for document annotation in chapter 6. Some available systems provide a simple text-mining-based text categorization, e.g., the TREX component of the SAP Enterprise Portal; a comparison to our approach is found in section 6.2. Techniques for *global searching* are covered in chapter 7, e.g., the Repository Framework by SAP. We propose the use of ontology-based metadata and a fuzzy search approach in chapter 8. Techniques for *integrating external applications* by means of portlets are discussed in chapter 9. Existing inter-portlet communication capabilities (e.g., the IBM Click-to-Action technology) are limited as they do not address the semantics of the transmitted information. The SAP Unification and Drag&Relate technology provides an interesting approach that also covers a semantic integration, however only for special Unifier iViews (see section 10.1). We present a generic approach for communicating the user context among portlets in chapter 10.

Chapter 4

Semantic Web Technologies

In the previous chapter enterprise knowledge portals have been identified as the solution of choice for addressing the unsatisfying integration of structured and unstructured information and its contextualization in enterprises (*awareness of problem*). The main idea of this work is that Semantic Web technologies can eliminate (or at least diminish) remaining deficiencies. This chapter gives an overview on those technologies that are then used within the actual design proposals in part II (*suggestion phase*).

In 1998 Tim Berners-Lee introduced his roadmap towards the Semantic Web [BL98]. His vision was that the existing World Wide Web should be enriched by metadata that would enable computers to understand the information given in web resources. If a machine was able to really understand the meaning a document it would be able to work with it, retrieve additional information, put it in a wider context, and communicate about it with other machines.

A main area where semantic metadata can bring improvement is searching. Most search engines on the Internet and within intranets work on the basis of fulltext keywords. Documents that are relevant to a user query are determined using so-called information retrieval models like the Vector Space Model [BYRN99] (for details see section 7.2). Despite the progress in this discipline, existing information retrieval approaches have their limits with respect to complex queries. In addition, a search engine cannot deal with the ambiguity of the language, i.e. differentiate between homographs/homonyms and polysemes[1]. For example, a query for the keyword "Jaguar" will find pages related to an animal, a car brand, a French fighter airplane, and a computer operating system.

Difficulties result mainly from the fact that the information on the World Wide Web can be read by machines; however, it cannot be understood by them. There are two approaches for solving this problem: One possibility is to try to enable machines to understand human language. The research area of natural language processing (NLP) emphasizes on this task. Today, NLP however provides no satisfying solutions for free text. Hence, a different approach needs to be considered. The idea of the Semantic Web is to prepare the information in such a way that it can be more easily understood by machines, i.e. the information must be supplemented by metadata with precise semantics. A descriptive model must be defined, that permits machines to exchange and process semantic information. We need a standardized metadata model and syn-

---

[1]*Homographs* are words which have one spelling but different pronunciations and meanings. Likewise, *homonyms* have one spelling, one pronunciation, but different unrelated meanings, which is what distinguishes them from *polysemes*, where all the meanings can be traced back to the same source [Hig05].

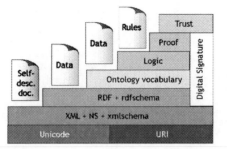

Figure 4.1: Layers of the Semantic Web [BL00]

tax, as well as the possibility to define a vocabulary for its interpretation (a so-called ontology) in order to be able to recognize connections between information elements and automatically draw logical conclusions.

As machines can then not only understand but also autonomously exchange information, Berners-Lee [BLHL01] has the vision of software agents that can act on behalf of humans. Agents will not only be able to recognize that a document contains certain keywords, but they will also understand their connections and relations. Hence, they can move from document to document or from application to application and to carry out orders on behalf of the user. A software agent could automatically make an appointment with a suitable attorney, find a restaurant that is suitable to the preferences of the user, compute the most favorable traffic route, etc. The Internet appearance of a law office will no longer only contain keywords such as attorney, law, etc., but inform the agent by using a certain language about the opening hours and agree with it upon a date for the appointment.

Berners-Lee claims that the Semantic Web will completely change the way we live our lives. However, before this can become reality, the necessary technical foundations are needed. Figure 4.1 shows an often used diagram, which represents the individual techniques that are developed within the Semantic Web activity of the World Wide Web Consortium (W3C)[2] as a "layer cake". The layers are dependent of each other and present the Semantic Web as a pyramid.

Documents on the Semantic Web contain metadata. Using an XML syntax, this metadata is encoded using the Resource Description Framework (RDF) [W3C04d] as the language for the description of resources and RDF Schema (RDFS) [W3C04c] for the definition of the metadata schema (see section 4.1). RDFS is based on a class concept and inheritance. Above this lies the ontology layer. An ontology is capable of describing "things", e.g., persons, that exist in a certain domain and relationships among them. These "things" can then also be used as a vocabulary for the metadata of resources. The standard for describing ontologies on the Semantic Web is the Web Ontology Language (OWL) [W3C04a], supporting richer semantics on top of RDFS (see section 4.2). The computation of ontologies, the merging, and the analysis is done in the logic layer. Information that exists only implicitly can be made explicit by menas of so-called reasoners or inference machines (see section 4.3).

The rest of the Semantic Web is still much of a field of research. Hence, even though the original vision aims at the whole of the Internet, Semantic Web technologies are so far more applicable to an enterprise setting, particularly as the still unsolved trust and proof issues (also in section 4.3) are easier to resolve.

---

[2]http://www.w3.org/2001/sw/

One ongoing research topic is information retrieval on the Semantic Web. In the original vision machines are communicating with other machines. Even though improved searching was one motivation for the Semantic Web, the communication between humans and machines is so far considered rather untouched by the existence of metadata. Today's Semantic Web techniques support no fuzzy searches and ranking of results. Human users are however used to work with ranked result lists that also contain information that does not "exactly" match their query. A similarity-based information retrieval approach for ontology-based metadata is presented in chapter 8.

4.1 Resource Description Framework (RDF)

The third layer of the Semantic Web pyramid, above Unicode, namespaces, and XML, is formed by the Resource Description Framework (RDF) and RDF Schema (RDFS). RDF is a relatively young recommendation by the World Wide Web Consortium (W3C) [W3C04d], which was originally developed for describing metadata of Web documents. RDF is however also suitable to represent data that is independent of other documents. RDF extends the only syntactically defined XML by formal semantics. RDF Schema [W3C04c] extends RDF by modeling concepts, just like XML Schema for XML.

Meanwhile tools for the storage and administration of RDF and RDFS data are available (e.g., Jena[3] and Sesame[4]). They provide a persistent storage for RDF data and support different access methods and formats. Query languages such as RDQL and RQL have evolved, which are finally leading to a standardized query language called SPARQL [W3C05].

4.1.1 RDF Model and Syntax

RDF is based on a simple triple-based model that follows the subject-predicate-object metaphor: *Resources* have a number of *properties* with specific *values*. Resources and properties are uniquely identified by a URI. The values can be literals or other resources (again identified by their URI). RDF uses a specific namespace `http://www.w3.org/1999/02/22-rdf-syntax-ns#` (usually abbreviated as `rdf:`) for URIs that represent concepts of the RDF model (e.g., `rdf:Description`, `rdf:type`).

In a graphical notation, RDF statements are depicted as directed graphs where the nodes are either resources (drawn as ovals) or literals (drawn as rectangles); the arcs represent the properties. Figure 4.2 shows a sample RDF graph that specifies title and creator of a resource, in this case a PDF document. The creator is further described by her name and as being an employee. Note that RDF uses URIs to identify:

- Resources, e.g., `http://www.inwiss.org/documents/FreeplaySolar-Radio.pdf`

- Other "things" (also represented as resources), e.g., `http://www.inwiss.org/ontology#Tina`

---

[3]`http://jena.sourceforge.net`
[4]`http://www.openrdf.org`

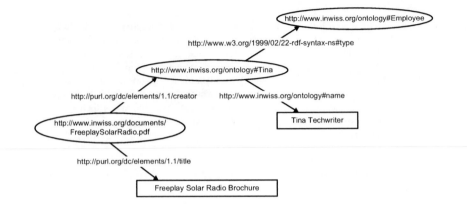

Figure 4.2: Sample RDF graph

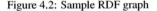

```
<?xml version="1.0"?>
<rdf:RDF xmlns:rdf="http://www.w3.org/1999/02/22-rdf-syntax-ns#"
  xmlns:dc="http://purl.org/dc/elements/1.1/"
  xmlns:onto="http://www.inwiss.org/ontology#">

<rdf:Description rdf:about=
  "http://www.inwiss.org/documents/FreeplaySolarRadio.pdf">
  <dc:title>Freeplay Solar Radio Brochure</dc:title>
  <dc:creator rdf:resource="http://www.inwiss.org/ontology#Tina"/>
</rdf:Description>

<onto:Employee rdf:about="http://www.inwiss.org/ontology#Tina">
  <onto:name>Tina Techwriter</onto:name>
</onto:Employee>

</rdf:RDF>
```

Figure 4.3: RDF example in RDF/XML syntax

- Kinds of things, e.g., `http://www.inwiss.org/ontology#Employee`

- Properties of those things, e.g., `http://www.inwiss.org/ontology#name`

In the example, the concepts `title` and `creator` were borrowed from the Dublin Core metadata standard [DCM03] (see chapter 5), `Emplyoee` and `name` are defined in the sample ontology below (see next section); this is indicated by the corresponding namespaces. In addition to URIs, RDF also uses character strings such as "Tina Techwriter" and values from other datatypes such as integers and dates, as the values of properties.

RDF provides an XML-based syntax (called RDF/XML) for metadata exchange. Figure 4.3 shows the same RDF example in RDF/XML syntax. Note that this RDF/XML also contains resources, as well as properties (using an XML namespace) and their respective values.

Like HTML, RDF/XML is machine processable and can link pieces of information across the Web by using URIs. However, unlike conventional hypertext, RDF URIs can refer to any identifiable thing, including things that may not be directly retrievable on the Web (such as the

```
@prefix rdf: <http://www.w3.org/1999/02/22-rdf-syntax-ns#> .
@prefix dc: <http://purl.org/dc/elements/1.1/> .
@prefix onto: <http://www.inwiss.org/ontology#> .

<http://www.inwiss.org/documents/FreeplaySolarRadio.pdf> dc:title
  "Freeplay Solar Radio Brochure" .
<http://www.inwiss.org/documents/FreeplaySolarRadio.pdf> dc:creator
  onto:Tina .

onto:Tina rdf:type onto:Employee .
onto:Tina onto:name "Tina Techwriter" .
```

Figure 4.4: RDF example in N3 notation

employee `Tina`). The result is that in addition to describing such things as webpages, RDF can also describe cars, businesses, people, news events, etc. In addition, RDF properties themselves have URIs, to precisely identify the relationships that exist between the linked items [W3C04b].

The RDF/XML syntax is very suitable for the processing of metadata by machines, however quite hard to read for humans, especially when getting started. Hence, Berners-Lee and Conolly [BLC03] define a simpler N3 notation as an alternative which also makes the triple model more apparent. Triples are represented as "sentences" terminated by a period; namespaces can be defined using the `@prefix` directive. The above example in N3 notation is shown in figure 4.4. Throughout this work we will use N3 instead of RDF/XML where appropriate for better readability.

4.1.2 RDF Schema

With a pure RDF model only links between resources or value assignments can be expressed. This is done on the basis of properties, there is however no mechanism for defining which properties can be used where. Therefore the W3C has made a further step towards a richer representation formalism by introducing simple ontological modeling primitives (classes, sub-classes, etc.) with RDF Schema (RDFS) [W3C04c].

RDF Schema provides the facilities needed to describe classes and properties, and to indicate which classes and properties are expected to be used together. In other words, RDF Schema provides a type system for RDF. The RDFS type system is in some respects similar to the type systems of object-oriented programming languages such as Java. For example, RDF Schema allows resources to be defined as instances of one or more classes. In addition, it allows classes to be organized in a hierarchical fashion. However, RDF classes and properties are in some respects also very different from programming language types. RDF class and property descriptions do not create a "straightjacket" into which information must be forced, but instead provide additional information about the RDF resources they describe [W3C04b].

The RDF Schema facilities are themselves provided in the form of an RDF vocabulary, i.e. as a specialized set of predefined RDF resources with their own special meanings. The resources in the RDFS vocabulary have URIs with the prefix `http://www.w3.org/2000/01/rdf-schema#` (or shortly `rdfs:`). Vocabulary descriptions (schemas) written in the RDFS language are legal RDF graphs.

A basic step in any description process is identifying the various kinds of things to be described. RDFS refers to these "kinds of things" as classes. A class in RDFS corresponds to the generic concept of a type or category, somewhat like the notion of a class in object-oriented programming languages. RDF classes can be used to represent almost any category of thing, such

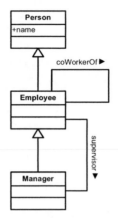

Figure 4.5: UML model for sample RDFS ontology

as webpages, people, document types, databases, or abstract concepts. Classes are described using the RDFS resource rdfs:Class.

Within this work we use a mail order company, which sells various consumer products via call centers as a scenario. For example, suppose we wanted to use RDF to provide information about the persons working for this company as shown in the UML model in figure 4.5 (for a model of the full scenario see appendix A.1). In RDF Schema, we would first need a class to represent the category of things that are persons. The resources that belong to a class are called its instances; the property rdf:type is used to link instances to their classes. After describing the class Person, we might want to describe additional classes representing various specialized kinds of persons, e.g., employees and managers. These classes can be described in the same way as class Person, by assigning a URI to each of them, and writing RDF statements defining these resources as classes. The specialization relationship between two classes is described using the predefined rdfs:subClassOf property.

In addition to the specific classes of things we also need to be able to describe specific properties that characterize those classes (such as supervisor to represent the supervisor of an employee). In RDF Schema, properties are described using the RDF class rdf:Property. RDFS also provides a vocabulary for describing how properties and classes are intended to be used together in RDF data. The rdfs:range property is used to indicate that the values of a particular property, e.g., supervisor, are instances of a designated class, e.g., Manager. In addition, it can also be used to indicate that the value of a property is given by a typed literal, for example, if we wanted to indicate that the property name had values from the XML Schema datatype xsd:string. The rdfs:domain property is used to indicate that a particular property applies to a designated class.

RDFS provides a way to specialize properties as well as classes. This specialization relationship between two properties is described using the predefined rdfs:subPropertyOf property. For example, if supervisor and coWorkerOf are both properties with the domain Employee, we could describe the fact that supervisor is a specialization of coWorkerOf. The meaning of this rdfs:subPropertyOf relationship is that if Calvin is a supervisor of Ian, then he is also considered as being his co-worker. All rdfs:range and rdfs:domain properties that apply to an RDF property also apply to each of its subproperties.

Figure 4.6 shows the RDF/XML of a sample RDFS ontology. Further helpful RDF Schema concepts exist, e.g., for describing resources with additional text. This is accomplished by means of the `rdfs:comment` and `rdfs:label` properties. The label is used to give to a resource a readable name the comment to give it a longer, more detailed description. Values in different languages can be provided.

4.2 Web Ontology Language (OWL)

The fourth layer of the Semantic Web covers ontologies. The term ontology originally represents a subdiscipline of philosophy and is defined as "a particular theory about being or reality" [Gru93]. In recent time the term ontology is also used in information technology. In this context it refers to a specific vocabulary for describing a certain part of reality together with a number of assumptions about the meaning of the vocabulary. An example is the WordNet[5] online lexical reference system. WordNet has the goal of grouping equivalent elements of the English language and hence describing semantic connections in the vocabulary. English nouns, verbs, adjectives, and adverbs are grouped by synonym relations, i.e. each group represents a certain lexical meaning.

> Heflin et al. [HHL02] state that "an ontology provides a particular perspective on the world or some part there of. Wheras a knowledge representation system specifies how to represent concepts, an ontology speciefies what concepts to represent and how they are interrelated. Most researchers agree that an ontology must include a vocabulary and corresponding definitions but it is difficult to achive a more detailed characterization. Typically, the vocabulary includes terms for classes and relations, whereas the definitions of these terms may be informal text or may be specified using a formal language like predicate logic. The advantage of formal definitions is that they allow a machine to perform much deeper reasoning; the disadvantage is that these definitions are much more difficult to construct."

Ontologies have been utilized within the areas of artificial intelligence, natural language processing, and, more recently, information integration, e-commerce, and knowledge management. With the help of ontologies domain knowledge can be made understandable and exchangeable [Fen01]. This makes ontologies interesting for the Semantic Web. With the help of formal semantics agents on the Semantic Web should be able to understand the meaning of resources and services. Working ontologies will be a key factor for the realization of the Semantic Web [Mae02].

In order to be able to implement ontologies on the Semantic Web, an expressive, uniform ontology language needs to be defined. The last section showed that RDF Schema already provides some simple ontological concepts. If machines are expected to perform useful reasoning tasks on the Semantic Web, an ontology language must, however, go beyond the basic semantics of RDFS. Hence, based on DAML+OIL[6], the Web Ontology Language (OWL) [W3C04a] has evolved as a formalism. OWL builds upon RDFS and extends it by additional concepts for describing properties and classes: among others, relations between classes (e.g., disjointness), cardinality (e.g., "exactly one"), equality, richer typing of properties, characteristics of properties (e.g., symmetry), and enumerated classes.

---

[5]http://wordnet.princeton.edu
[6]http://www.daml.org

```
<?xml version="1.0"?>
<!DOCTYPE rdf:RDF [<!ENTITY xsd "http://www.w3.org/2001/XMLSchema#">]>
<rdf:RDF xmlns:rdf="http://www.w3.org/1999/02/22-rdf-syntax-ns#"
  xmlns:rdfs="http://www.w3.org/2000/01/rdf-schema#"
  xml:base="http://www.inwiss.org/ontology">

<rdfs:Class rdf:ID="Person"/>

<rdfs:Class rdf:ID="Employee"/>
  <rdfs:subClassOf rdf:resource="#Person"/>
</rdfs:Class>

<rdfs:Class rdf:ID="Manager">
  <rdfs:subClassOf rdf:resource="#Employee"/>
</rdfs:Class>

<rdf:Property rdf:ID="name">
  <rdfs:domain rdf:resource="#Person"/>
  <rdfs:range rdf:resource="&xsd;string"/>
</rdf:Property>

<rdf:Property rdf:ID="coWorkerOf">
  <rdfs:domain rdf:resource="#Employee"/>
  <rdfs:range rdf:resource="#Employee"/>
</rdf:Property>

<rdf:Property rdf:ID="supervisor">
  <rdfs:subPropertyOf rdf:resource="#coWorkerOf"/>
  <rdfs:domain rdf:resource="#Employee"/>
  <rdfs:range rdf:resource="#Manager"/>
</rdf:Property>

<Manager rdf:ID="Calvin">
  <name>Calvin Rosie</name>
</Manager>

<Employee rdf:ID="Ian">
  <name>Ian Benner</name>
  <supervisor rdf:resource="#Calvin"/>
</Employee>.

<Employee rdf:ID="Sean">
  <name>Sean McClain</name>
  <supervisor rdf:resource="#Calvin"/>
  <coWorkerOf rdf:resource="#Ian"/>
</Employee>

</rdf:RDF>
```

Figure 4.6: Sample RDFS ontology in RDF/XML

Like for RDF(S) the support of OWL through standard software tools is growing. Graphical ontology editors (e.g., Protege[7] with its OWL plug-in) and reasoners are becoming available.

4.2.1 Sublanguages of OWL

OWL provides three increasingly expressive sublanguages designed for use by specific communities of implementers and users [W3C04a]:

- *OWL Lite* supports those users primarily needing a classification hierarchy and simple constraints. It is simpler to provide tool support for OWL Lite than its more expressive relatives; it has a lower formal complexity than OWL DL.

- *OWL DL* supports those users who want the maximum expressiveness while retaining computational completeness (all conclusions are guaranteed to be computable) and decidability (all computations will finish in finite time). OWL DL includes all language constructs of OWL Full, but they can be used only under certain restrictions. It is named OWL DL due to its correspondence with description logics that form its formal foundation.

- *OWL Full* is meant for users who want maximum expressiveness and the syntactic freedom of RDF with no computational guarantees. For example, in OWL Full a class can be treated simultaneously as a collection of individuals and as an individual itself. OWL Full allows an ontology to augment the meaning of the pre-defined (RDF or OWL) vocabulary. It is unlikely that any reasoning software will be able to support complete reasoning for every feature of OWL Full.

Each of these sublanguages is an extension of its simpler predecessor, both in what can be legally expressed and in what can be validly concluded. Ontology developers adopting OWL should consider which sublanguage best suits their needs. For the purposes of this work basic expressiveness is sufficient. Hence, the following subsection will present the concepts of OWL Lite in detail and only shortly comment on the extensions in OWL DL and Full.

4.2.2 OWL Lite Language Concepts

As mentioned above, OWL builds upon RDF Schema. Hence, the constructs `rdfs:Class`, `rdfs:subClassOf`, `rdf:Property`, `rdfs:subPropertyOf`, `rdfs:range`, and `rdfs:domain` also apply to OWL.

Note that OWL DL and OWL Lite introduce an own `owl:Class` which is defined as a subclass of `rdfs:Class`. The rationale for having a separate class construct lies in restrictions on OWL DL and OWL Lite, which imply that not all RDFS classes are legal OWL DL classes. Instances of OWL classes are called individuals. When it comes to properties, unlike RDFS, OWL explicitly distinguishes between object properties (with individuals as values) and datatype properties (with literal values). Both `owl:ObjectProperty` and `owl:DatatypeProperty` are defined as subclasses of `rdf:Property`.

Consider the extended version of the sample UML model in figure 4.7). The OWL language constructs used in the diagram as stereotypes are described in the following. In order to provide means for ontological mapping, OWL Lite offers the following features related to equality or inequality [W3C04a]:

---

[7]`http://protege.stanford.edu`

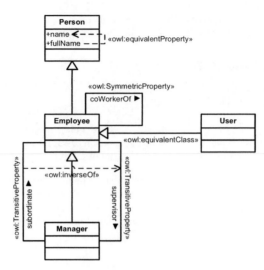

Figure 4.7: Extended UML model (sample OWL ontology)

- owl:equivalentClass: Two classes may be stated to be equivalent. Equivalent classes have the same instances. Equality can be used to create synonymous classes. For example, Employee can be stated to be owl:equivalentClass to User (of an application system). From this a reasoner can deduce that any individual that is an instance of Employee is also an instance of User and vice versa.

- owl:equivalentProperty: Two properties may be stated to be equivalent. Equivalent properties relate one individual to the same set of other individuals or literals. Equality may be used to create synonymous properties. For example, name may be stated to be an owl:equivalentProperty to fullName.

- owl:sameAs: Two individuals may be stated to be the same. These constructs may be used to create a number of different names that refer to the same individual. For example, the individual Larry may be stated to be the same individual as BigBoss.

- owl:differentFrom: An individual may be stated to be different from other individuals. For example, the individual Calvin may be stated to be different from the individual Tina. Explicitly stating that individuals are different can be important as OWL does not necessarily assume that individuals have one and only one name.

- owl:AllDifferent: A number of individuals may be stated to be mutually distinct in one owl:AllDifferent statement. For example, Calvin, Tina, and Ian could be stated to be mutually distinct using the owl:AllDifferent construct.

Likewise, there are special identifiers in OWL Lite that are used to provide information concerning properties and their values [W3C04a]:

- owl:inverseOf: One property may be stated to be the inverse of another property. If the property P is stated to be the inverse of the property Q, then if X is related to Y by the Q property, then Y is related to X by the P property. For example, if subordinate is the inverse of supervisor and Ian has a supervisor value of Calvin, then a reasoner can deduce that Calvin has a subordinate named Ian.

- owl:TransitiveProperty: Properties may be stated to be transitive. If a property is transitive, then if the pair (x,y) is connected by the transitive property P and the pair (y,z) is connected by P then the pair (x,z) is also connected by P. For example, if supervisor is stated to be transitive and if Larry is supervisor of Calvin and Calvin is a supervisor of Ian, then a reasoner can deduce that King is supervsor of Ian.

- owl:SymmetricProperty: Properties may be stated to be symmetric. If a property is symmetric, then if the symmetric property P applies to the pair (x,y) then P also applies to the pair (y,x). For example, coWorkerOf may be stated to be a symmetric property. Given that Ian is coWorkerOf the individual Sean a reasoner can then deduce that Sean is coWorkerOf the individual Ian.

Figure 4.8 shows the extended OWL version of the RDFS ontology from figure 4.6 in N3 notation. By using the above OWL definitions, a reasoner can deduce certain implicit information and infer the additional triples shown in figure 4.9.

In addition to the above, properties in OWL Lite may be stated to have only a single value by defining them as an owl:FunctionalProperty, which is a shorthand for stating that the property's maximum cardinality is 1 (see below). In addition they may be defined to be an owl:InverseFunctionalProperty. This characteristic can be compared to the concept of unique or primary keys in database systems. For example, ssn (referring to a social security number) may be stated to be inverse functional. The inverse of this property has at most one value for any individual in the class of social security numbers.

OWL Lite allows restrictions to be placed on how properties can be used by instances of a class. The available range restrictions are owl:allValuesFrom and owl:someValues-From; the cardinality restrictions are owl:minCardinality, owl:maxCardinality, and owl: cardinality (in OWL Lite however limited to cardinalities of value 0 or 1). Finally, OWL Lite contains an owl:intersectionOf constructor that allows intersections of classes and restrictions (but also limits its usage compared to OWL DL and OWL Full). Restrictions are not used throughout this work, hence, refer to [W3C04a] for details.

Additional constructs of the OWL DL and OWL Full vocabulary that extend OWL Lite are owl:oneOf, owl:hasValue, owl:disjointWith, owl:unionOf, owl:complementOf, and complex classes. Both OWL DL and OWL Full use the same vocabulary although OWL DL is subject to some restrictions. Roughly, OWL DL requires type separation (a class cannot also be an individual or property, a property cannot also be an individual or class). This implies that restrictions cannot be applied to the OWL language elements themselves (something that is allowed in OWL Full) [W3C04a].

OWL uses the RDF mechanisms for data values, i.e. like for RDF the built-in OWL datatypes are largely taken from the XML Schema datatypes. In addition, OWL supports notions of ontology inclusion and relationships and attaching information to ontologies. It allows annotations on classes, properties, individuals and ontology headers. RDF already has a small vocabulary for describing versioning information; OWL significantly extends this vocabulary.

4.3 Logic, Proof, and Trust

The remaining part of the Semantic Web is still subject to ongoing research and so far only partly standardized. The fifth layer of the architecture is the logic layer. On top of ontologies

```
@prefix rdf: <http://www.w3.org/1999/02/22-rdf-syntax-ns#> .
@prefix rdfs: <http://www.w3.org/2000/01/rdf-schema#> .
@prefix owl: <http://www.w3.org/2002/07/owl#> .
@prefix xsd: <http://www.w3.org/2001/XMLSchema#> .
@prefix : <http://www.inwiss.org/ontology#> .

:Person rdf:type owl:Class .

:Employee rdf:type owl:Class .
:Employee rdfs:subClassOf :Person .

:Manager rdf:type owl:Class .
:Manager rdfs:subClassOf :Employee .

:name rdf:type owl:DatatypeProperty .
:name rdfs:domain :Person .
:name rdfs:range xsd:string .
:name owl:equivalentProperty :fullName .

:coWorkerOf rdf:type owl:SymmetricProperty .
:coWorkerOf rdfs:domain :Employee .
:coWorkerOf rdfs:range :Employee .

:supervisor rdf:type owl:TransitiveProperty .
:supervisor rdfs:subPropertyOf :coWorker .
:supervisor rdfs:domain :Employee .
:supervisor rdfs:range :Manager .

:subordinate rdf:type owl:TransitiveProperty .
:subordinate rdfs:domain :Manager .
:subordinate rdfs:range :Employee .
:subordinate owl:inverseOf :supervisor .

:Larry rdf:type :Manager .
:Larry :name "Larry King" .
:Larry :sameAs :BigBoss .

:Calvin rdf:type :Manager .
:Calvin :name "Calvin Rosie" .
:Calvin :supervisor :Larry .

:Ian rdf:type :Employee .
:Ian :name "Ian Benner" .
:Ian :supervisor :Calvin .

:Sean rdf:type :Employee .
:Sean :name "Sean McClain" .
:Sean :supervisor :Calvin .
:Sean :coWorkerOf :Ian .
```

Figure 4.8: Sample OWL ontology in N3 notation

```
@prefix rdf: <http://www.w3.org/1999/02/22-rdf-syntax-ns#> .
@prefix rdfs: <http://www.w3.org/2000/01/rdf-schema#> .
@prefix owl: <http://www.w3.org/2002/07/owl#> .
@prefix xsd: <http://www.w3.org/2001/XMLSchema#> .
@prefix : <http://www.inwiss.org/ontology#> .
```

```
:Larry rdf:type :Employee .          :Ian rdf:type :Person .
:Larry rdf:type :Person .            :Ian rdf:type :User .
:Larry rdf:type :User .              :Ian :fullName "Ian Benner" .
:Larry :fullName "Larry King" .      :Ian :supervisor :Larry .
:Larry :subordinate :Calvin .        :Ian :supervisor :BigBoss .
:Larry :subordinate :Ian .           :Ian :coWorkerOf :Calvin .
:Larry :subordinate :Sean .          :Ian :coWorkerOf :Larry .
:Larry :coWorkerOf :Calvin .         :Ian :coWorkerOf :BigBoss .
:Larry :coWorkerOf :Ian .            :Ian :coWorkerOf :Sean
:Larry :coWorkerOf :Sean .

                                     :Sean rdf:type :Person .
:BigBoss rdf:type :Manager .         :Sean rdf:type :User .
:BigBoss rdf:type :Employee .        :Sean :fullName "Sean McClain" .
:BigBoss rdf:type :Person .          :Sean :supervisor :Larry .
:BigBoss rdf:type :User .            :Sean :supervisor :BigBoss .
:BigBoss :name "Larry King" .        :Sean :coWorkerOf :Calvin .
:BigBoss :fullName "Larry King" .    :Sean :coWorkerOf :Larry .
:BigBoss :sameAs :Larry .            :Sean :coWorkerOf :BigBoss .
:BigBoss :subordinate :Calvin .
:BigBoss :subordinate :Ian .
:BigBoss :subordinate :Sean .
:BigBoss :coWorkerOf :Calvin .
:BigBoss :coWorkerOf :Ian .
:BigBoss :coWorkerOf :Sean .

:Calvin rdf:type :Employee .
:Calvin rdf:type :Person .
:Calvin rdf:type :User .
:Calvin :fullName "Calvin Rosie" .
:Calvin :supervisor :BigBoss .
:Calvin :subordinate :Ian .
:Calvin :subordinate :Sean .
:Calvin :coWorkerOf :Larry .
:Calvin :coWorkerOf :BigBoss .
:Calvin :coWorkerOf :Ian .
:Calvin :coWorkerOf :Sean .
```

Figure 4.9: Inferred triples from sample ontology

with concepts such as subclasses, transitive and inverse properties, etc., logical principles and rules need to be specified, which allow to draw conclusions and make deductions. Such rules are called also inference rules. In the previous section transitive properties were explained by using a supervisor property as an example. The fact that we can conclude that Larry is the supervisor of Ian is a result of inference rules. It is the task of an inference engine to implement these rules in a way such that new knowledge is generated from the existing data. While the semantics of transitive properties are an example for a simple inference rule built into OWL, more complex custom rules will be required for a fully functional Semantic Web. A proposal based on the Rule Markup Language (RuleML)[8], which has been submitted to the World Wide Web Consortium for standardization, is the Semantic Web Rule Language (SWRL) [DAM03].

After additional knowledge has been generated with the help of inference rules, it is the task of the sixth layer to prove that this knowledge is actually true. It can be expected that agents need to follow various semantic links in order to make their conclusions and that certain inferences will be based on already inferred knowledge [SH01]. Hence, it might be rather difficult to provide such proofs. A main problem besides the mathematical provability is the question whether the knowledge collected by the agents is trustworthy. It is thus up to the seventh layer to clarify how much confidence can be put into the data on the Semantic Web. For this purpose digital signatures are envisioned to be used on all levels of the Semantic Web, e.g., for signing RDF metadata. Based on a web of trust, in which the user specifies which sources he/she trusts, an agent can then derive how trustworthy a collected piece of information is.

Signing RDF data is however not as straightforward as it might seem. One might think that XML Signature [W3C02] techniques simply need to be applied to an RDF/XML document. However, XML Signature uses an XML canonicalization method in order to unify potentially different representations of the same data. The same RDF can however be represented in XML in different ways. Hence a special RDF canonicalization method (such as presented by Carroll [Car03b]) is required.

The spreading of the digital signature has not yet made as much progress as it was expected some years ago. It is not easy to predict whether and when digital signatures as well as the necessary public key infrastructures will be widely implemented. If one regards however the structure and the goal of the Semantic Web, it becomes clear that the digital signature is an important component of it. After all, only trusted information is useful. Perhaps, the digital signature will experience a renaissance through the possible progress of the Semantic Web.

---

[8]http://www.ruleml.org

Part II

State-of-the-Art and Proposed Extensions

Chapter 5

Metadata for Content and Structure Management

As elaborated in chapter 3, key services provided by enterprise knowledge portals are content and structure management. As part of the *suggestion phase* of the research effort presented in this work, this chapter covers state-of-practice building blocks of the proposed design in these areas. The role of metadata and the applicability of Semantic Web technologies are discussed, proposing the use of a simple hierarchical taxonomy for navigation and an ontology for semantic searching. The required manual annotation of (textual) documents is identified as a major open issue which is then addressed by a novel proposal in the next chapter.

This alternating fashion of presenting state-of-the-art and scientific contribution in consecutive chapters is also pursued for the areas of global searching and the integration of external content and applications in chapters 7−10.

The central element of content management is "content". In the broadest sense the term content covers the entire range of information of an enterprise – texts, pictures, diagrams, database data, etc. – no matter in which format and where it is stored. As a demarcation to the term information, content can be understood as exchangeable information objects or packages. Characteristics of content are its structure, formatting, layout, and media format. Content management can be defined as the systematic and target-oriented handling of content. That means that the same content can be structured, represented, and offered in different ways for different target groups [FG02]. In the reference architecture of enterprise knowledge portals presented in chapter 3, the content management service is accompanied by a structure management service which is responsible for the portal navigation. Managing the content navigation is also a core feature of content management systems (CMS) which is why both services are covered together in this chapter.

The term content management is closely related to the term knowledge management (see chapter 2). The terms are often falsely used as synonyms; knowledge management however reaches far beyond content management. The interdependencies of the two terms lie in the fact that knowledge management without content is not possible. Explicit knowledge is actually content, which has to be managed through content management. Roughly, content management can be seen as a subset of knowledge management. It puts all useful content of an enterprise at the disposal of the employees. With the help of this content they can then produce knowledge, which is likewise prepared and published by content management. Knowledge management has the task of generating knowledge through a corporate culture and by motivating the employees. Content management can take over the part of the knowledge distribution [Bs99].

Historically, the term content management has evolved from the need to organize the creation and management of web content (web content management). Web-based technologies have become a key technology for fulfilling business processes, e.g., as a distribution channel, or for publishing information within an organization. In both cases (for external and internal use) the information becomes more and more dynamic. In the past mainly static HTML pages were created and managed by a small number of people. Today, a manual management of webpages is almost impossible. In addition to its highly dynamic nature, the content is usually provided by sources with only little knowledge in HTML and web technologies, e.g., operating departments of an enterprise.

Many concepts of content management have, however, already been used for non-web resources before. Document management systems (DMS) have been employed to manage the overload of documents that are created within an enterprise. This involves textual (e.g., office) documents but also non-textual ones, e.g., technical drawings. With the emerging awareness for knowledge management the terms (web) content and document management have converged. Many content management systems nowadays provide functionality for managing HTML-based content as well as other documents.

5.1   Content Management Systems

The major task of content management is the structuring and administration of content. In addition, it concerns searching the sources of the enterprise for content, the designation of its relevance, and its storage. Koop et al. [KJvO01, p. 14] name the tasks of content management as:

- Creation and editing of content (identification of existing relevant and creation of new content)

- Administration of content (structuring, indexing, and filtering)

- Distribution and presentation of content (based on role definitions, e.g., author, publisher, and administrator)

- Providing use and processing possibilities (interpretation and application, but also evaluation, commentating, and extension of the content)

Content does not appear or disappear coincidentally, but follows a content lifecycle [Ger02]. Even though there is no generally accepted definition, it usually consists of planning, acquisition/creation, verification, publishing, revision, and archiving phases (see figure 5.1). Content management systems support this content lifecycle by providing among others authoring and workflow functionality.

A content management system (CMS) is an IT-based tool for the organization, administration, and realization of content management [KJvO01, p. 16]. Today's content management systems are able to digitally produce, store, search for, and re-use content of various types. Web content management systems (WCMS) have the particular advantage that users can maintain web content without HTML knowledge. The separation of structure, layout, and raw content as well as the administration of structure and representation are the core requirements for a flexible WCMS. As mentioned above, the technologies have converged especially in the context of enterprise knowledge portals, which are usually capable of managing (web) content that can

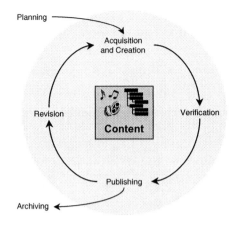

Figure 5.1: Content lifecycle [Ger02]

be viewed (and edited) within the portal as well as documents that require special application systems.

According to Ehlers [Ehl02] content management systems consist of the following six main components:

- *Asset management* is the main service of a CMS providing a content repository as a central storage. Besides elementary functions for storage, search, and access also archiving and versioning is offered [Ehl02, p. 113]. Multi user access is supported through a locking machanism: By means of a so-called check-out, editors can mark content they wish to work on; it becomes locked until it is checked-in again. Thereby versioning can be easily realized as well. Editing, i.e. the creation and modification, of (web) content represents a further central task of a CMS, as it must be usable also by employees without HTML knowledge.

- *Permission management* regulates the user-dependent access to the content. The main requirement is the examination of the user and his permissions for using certain functions, e.g., creating, viewing, changing and removing content. A prerequisite for an authorization is the registration and identification (login) of the users. In portal systems user and permission management is provided by the personalzation and security base service (see section 3.2).

- *Workflow control* it implements the content lifecycle by automating and coordinating the content management activities [Ehl02, p. 118], providing a basis for decentralized and parallel working. A workflow describes the way a document takes from its first draft to its final publishing, with the persons entitled for the individual steps being defined by the permission management. Beyond workflow, a CMS usually offers workgroup functionality, e.g., notification emails for responsible administrators or authors.

- *Import and export management* allows the integration of external data sources and content providers. An automated exchange of content between different websites and the integration of external content components (in particular news messages) into a website is designated as content syndication; it is usually based on the RSS[1] format. In portal systems content syndication is mostly performed by means of specific RSS portlets (for details see section 9.1).

- The *template management* is important for the separation of content and layout (regarding web content). In this context a template is a structured substitute for content, which is filled with concrete content through instantiation [KJvO01, p. 79]. By menas of templates the same content can be represented in several different layouts and formats (e.g., for specific target groups).

- *Link management* deals with the navigation structure of the content stored in the system. For web content it also ensures a hassle-free navigation through the pages and reduces the probability of "dead links", as the hyperlinks within the content repository can be automatically examined for accessibility [Ehl02, p. 125]. In portal systems the link navigation within web content has to be coordinated with the portal navigation as provided by the structure management base service (see section 3.2).

In addition to the above Koop et al. [KJvO01] define the classification of content, maintaining metadata, as well as search mechanisms that permit searches on metadata and fulltext, as additional functionalities of CMS. The idea of metadata is to enrich the resources with additional, describing information which is readable and understandable both by humans and machines. The metadata represents a markup or classification of the resources. This is particularly useful for non-textual resources, however also text documents profit from a semantic annotation.

5.2   Metadata Standards

Metadata has been used for decades (e.g., in document management systems), however in the past the approaches were proprietary and the interoperability was limited. Meanwhile, with the emergence of the Semantic Web [BLHL01], a number of standards for the storage and administration of metadata has evolved.

As elaborated in chapter 4, the Resource Description Framework (RDF) [W3C04d] defines a standardized, XML-based form for representing metadata. RDF extends the only syntactically defined XML by formal semantics. For this purpose it uses a simple triple-based model: Resources are uniquely identified by a URI and have a number of properties with specific values. The values can be literals or other resources (again identified by their URI). RDF Schema [W3C04c] extends RDF by modeling concepts.

While RDF only defines the base model, i.e. the fact that resources can have properties with values, RDF Schema allows to more precisely specify the metadata elements which can be used. However, this must be done individually for each application domain. In order to allow for interoperability it is desirable to specify certain universal metadata elements as a kind of base vocabulary. This is what the Dublin Core Metadata Initiative[2] tries to achieve. The aim of Dublin Core is to standardize a determined number of metadata elements that can be used to annotate text documents and other resources.

Meanwhile many domain-specific metadata standards have come up, e.g., IMS Global Learning Consortium[3]. Dublin Core has its roots in the World Wide Web and in the area of digital

---

[1]RSS is an XML-based exchange format for content. Depending on the version, RSS stands for "RDF Site Summary", "Really Simple Syndication", or "Rich Site Summary"; for details see chapter 9.

[2]http://www.dublincore.org

[3]http://www.imsglobal.org

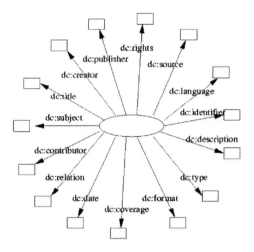

Figure 5.2: The Dublin Core hedgehog model [DCM02]

libraries. The metadata set is, however, rather application-independent, which is why we base the examples in this work (and our prototype) on Dublin Core. The concepts can however also be transferred to other models. The standard specifies fifteen elements, whose semantics were defined by an international and interdisciplinary group of experts. These elements are shown in figure 5.2 as an RDF graph, as the most common form of representation for Dublin Core metadata is RDF. The Dublin Core elements are identified by the namespace http://purl.org/dc/elements/1.1/. For example, the element "subject" is defined as http://purl.org/dc/elements/1.1/subject (or briefly dc:subject).

In the area of content and knowledge management (and for the purpose of this work) the following elements are of particular interest [DCM03]:

- dc:title: The title is the name under which the resource is known, e.g., the headline of a document.

- dc:creator: The creator is the entity that is responsible for the creation of the resource. This can be a person or an organization. If possible, a directory of possible creators with a unique identifier (e.g., LDAP/X.500 distinguished names) should be used as a value set; in an enterprise setting, the possible creators should be included in the enterprise ontology (see below).

- dc:subject: The subject or topic is usually specified using a set of keywords or by means of a classification scheme or taxonomy.

- dc:description: The description summarizes the content of the resource, e.g., by an abstract or table of contents.

- dc:date: The element dc:date is supposed to define an event in the life cycle of the resource, usually the date of creation or publication. The encoding of the date should be based on the ISO 8601 profile and the "YYYY-MM-DD" date format.

- dc:type: The element dc:type specifies the type or genre of the content of the resource. Also here a controlled vocabulary, i.e. a predefined set of possible types, should be used.

- dc:format: The format describes the physical or digital manifestation of the resource. It should reveal which hard and software is required for viewing or processing the content of the resource. MIME types (Multipurpose Internet Mail Extensions) have evolved as a standard for this purpose.

- dc:language: The language of the content of the resource should be specified using RFC 3066 and ISO 639, i.e. two or three letter language tags with optional subtags (e.g., "en-US" for US English).

- dc:coverage: The element dc:coverage designates the extent of the resource; Dublin Core names geographic coordinates and temporal periods as examples. In an enterprise context however also different possible "objects" can be found, e.g., products or departments.

Where possible a controlled vocabulary should be used as the set of possible values instead of free text. The element dc:subject is usually specified using a pre-defined number of keywords or a taxonomy. The use of an ontology as controlled vocabulary seems appropriate for dc:coverage.

It is difficult to clearly distinguish the terms taxonomy and ontology. A taxonomy is sometimes seen as a "simple ontology" or as a subset of an ontology [McG02]. In this work we use the terminology as follows: A *taxonomy* represents a hierarchical structure mainly for browsing and navigation support. An *ontology* on the other hand formally describes a part of the world; the completeness and machine processability are of particular interest. The annotation of documents with ontology elements supports semantic searching rather than navigation (see below).

5.3 Taxonomies for Navigation

A common approach for organizing documents and other resources is the use of a taxonomy. A taxonomy consists of a hierarchically ordered number of categories; the hierarchy is represented using generalization (or is-a) relations [HHL02].

Heflin et al. [HHL02] state that "the collection of is-a links specifies a partial order on classes; this order is often called a taxonomy or categorization hierarchy. The taxonomy can be used to generalize a concept to a more abstract class or to specialize a class to its more specific concepts. [...] Taxonomies clearly aid users in locating relevant information on the Web."

McGuinness [McG02] regards taxonomies as "simple ontologies" (see above) and states that "they provide a *controlled vocabulary* for their domain. [...] A simple taxonomy may be used for *site organization and navigation support*. Many websites today expose the top levels of a generalization hierarchy of terms as a kind of browsing structure. [...] Taxonomies may be used to support *expectation setting*. [...] If they [users] may explore even the top-level categories of the site's hierarchy, they can quickly determine if the site might have content (and/or services) of interest to them."

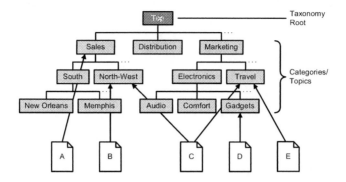

Figure 5.3: Classifying documents using a thematic taxonomy

A resource (document or service) is assigned to one or more taxonomy categories. A category can thus be seen as a kind of virtual directory that contains all resources on a certain topic. This approach is also used in web directories like Yahoo![4] or DMOZ[5] which try to structure the World Wide Web by means of a taxonomy. The user can browse the taxonomy and view the documents that are assigned to the individual categories.

An excerpt of a sample taxonomy is shown in figure 5.3. We use a mail order company, which sells various consumer products via call center as a scenario. The first taxonomy level consists of "Sales", "Distribution", and "Marketing". While the category "Sales" is geographically subdivided, the refinement within "Marketing" is based on the products of the enterprise. Documents can be assigned to taxonomy categories by means of metadata, e.g., in RDF using the Dublin Core element dc:subject.

RDF can also be used to describe a taxonomy. This approach is also pursued by DMOZ[6]. The individual categories are represented as resources identified by a URI; the hierarchical layout of the URIs reflects the hierarchy of the taxonomy. For example, the category "Audio" in figure 5.3 could be coded as http://www.inwiss.org/topics/Marketing/ Electronics/Audio. An excerpt of the sample taxonomy encoded in RDF is shown in figure 5.4.

5.4   Ontologies for Semantic Searching

In enterprise knowledge portals taxonomies are usually used for navigation purposes as a kind of menu structure. The simplicity and comprehensibility are therefore of particular importance. In order to completely describe the content of a resource (e.g., with the Dublin Core element dc:coverage) to allow semantic (in particular context-based) searching, more complex structures are necessary. We propose the use of an enterprise ontology for this purpose, i.e. a formal description of the concepts (products, customers, departments, employees, etc.) that are of interest to the enterprise. The term ontology has already been introduced in chapter 4; as mentioned above, its demarcation from the term taxonomy is rather difficult. Compared to a taxonomy an ontology is more complex and usually contains a larger number of instances.

---

[4]http://www.yahoo.com
[5]http://www.dmoz.org
[6]DMOZ RDF dumps are available at http://rdf.dmoz.org

```
<?xml version="1.0"?>
<!DOCTYPE rdf:RDF [<!ENTITY top "http://www.inwiss.org/topics/">]>
<rdf:RDF xmlns:rdf="http://www.w3.org/1999/02/22-rdf-syntax-ns#"
  xmlns:dc="http://purl.org/dc/elements/1.1/"
  xmlns:inwiss="http://www.inwiss.org/schema#">

<inwiss:Topic rdf:about="&top;">
  <dc:title>Top</dc:title>
  <inwiss:narrow rdf:resource="&top;Sales"/>
  <inwiss:narrow rdf:resource="&top;Distribution"/>
  <inwiss:narrow rdf:resource="&top;Marketing"/>
</inwiss:Topic>

<inwiss:Topic rdf:about="&top;Sales">
  <dc:title>Sales</dc:title>
  <inwiss:narrow rdf:resource="&top;Sales/South"/>
  <inwiss:narrow rdf:resource="&top;Sales/NorthWest"/>
  ...
</inwiss:Topic>

<inwiss:Topic rdf:about="&top;Sales/South">
  <dc:title>South</dc:title>
  <inwiss:narrow rdf:resource="&top;Sales/South/NewOrleans"/>
  ...
</inwiss:Topic>

...

</rdf:RDF>
```

Figure 5.4: Sample taxonomy encoded in RDF

> As opposed to taxonomies (or "simple ontologies") McGuinnes [McG02] states
> that "more structured ontologies may be able to provide *interoperability*. Con-
> trolled vocabularies enhance interoperability support, since different users and ap-
> plications are using the same set of terms. [...] More structured ontologies may be
> used to *support validation and verification testing* of data (and schemas). [...] More
> structured ontologies can support *structured, comparative, and customized search.*"

Based on DAML+OIL[7] the Web Ontology Language (OWL) [W3C04a] has evolved as a formalism for representing ontologies (see chapter 4). OWL builds upon on RDF Schema (see
above) and extends it by additional constructs. Classes and corresponding instances are defined. The classes follow an inheritance hierarchy, for example "Person" with "Customer" and
"Employee" as subclasses. The instances in the ontology represent the objects of interest in
the regarded domain (in this case the enterprise); they serve as possible values for the semantic annotation of resources. We propose to use the Dublin Core element `dc:coverage` for
linking resources to elements from an ontology which can then be used for semantic searches.
This way, we achive a clear separation to the taxonomy topics (assigned as `dc:subject`) that
are used mainly for navigation support (although it of course also possible to search for them).
While resources will be assigned to one or few taxonomy categories, their extent can cover a
much larger number of ontology instances. In addition, as mentioned above, we propose to
include the potential authors of resources (specified using `dc:creator`) in the ontology.

Our semantic annotation approach is summarized in the UML diagram in figure 5.5 which
also shows a small excerpt of the ontology of our scenario (with product items, subcategories,
categories, as well as employees and customers). The full ontology of the scenario is given in
appendix A.1, excerpts in RDF/N3 can be found in chapters 4 and 8. As mentioned above, a
taxonomy is sometimes seen as part of an ontology. As we use the same (RDF/OWL) approach
to represent both the taxonomy and the ontology, the taxonomy is also shown as part of the
ontology in the diagram. However, note that the taxonomy topics are completely independent
of the other ontology elements.

Figure 5.6 shows the metadata of a sample resource using the above Dublin Core elements
as an RDF graph; the corresponding RDF/XML encoding is given in figure 8.1. Apart from
literals, categories from a taxonomy and instances from an ontology are used as values. The
resource represents a PDF document (`dc:format`) titled "Freeplay Solar Radio Brochure"
(`dc:title`), created on April 4, 1998 (`dc:date`). The semantic annotation comprises classifying the document as belonging to the "Marketing / Electronics / Audio" topic from a taxonomy (`dc:subject`) and as dealing with the Freeplay Solar Radio product instance from an
ontology (`dc:coverage`). The document was created by the employee "Tina".

5.5   Summary

This chapter discussed the use of metadata and Semantic Web technologies for content and
structure management in enterprise portals. As mentioned above, most of today's systems use
metadata to manage and structure the content. This applies to stand-alone content management
systems as well as portal platforms with content management functionality. Usually a pre-
defined set of metadata elements (e.g., title, author, etc.) is provided, sometimes based on standards like Dublin Core, however usually free text is used as values. The classification using a
simple hierarchical taxonomy for navigation purposes can be regarded as state-of-practice (e.g.,
used by the SAP Enterprise Portal, see sections 3.4 and 6.2). We have proposed a dual approach

---

[7]`http://www.daml.org`

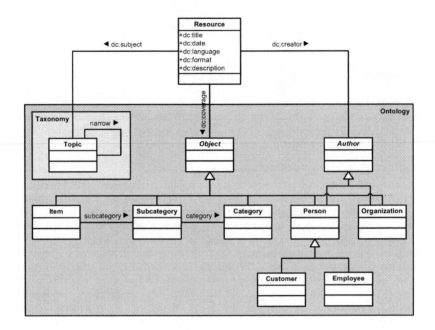

Figure 5.5: Annotation with taxonomy topics and ontology elements

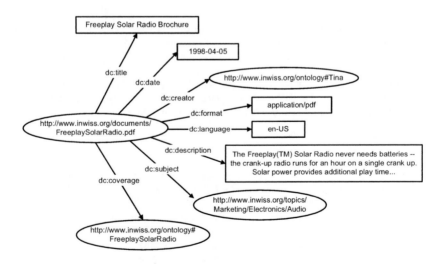

Figure 5.6: RDF metadata of a sample document

```
<?xml version="1.0"?>
<!DOCTYPE rdf:RDF [<!ENTITY top "http://www.inwiss.org/topics/">]>
<rdf:RDF xmlns:rdf="http://www.w3.org/1999/02/22-rdf-syntax-ns#"
  xmlns:dc="http://purl.org/dc/elements/1.1/"
  xml:base="http://www.inwiss.org/ontology">

<rdf:Description rdf:about=
  "http://www.inwiss.org/documents/FreeplaySolarRadio.pdf">
<dc:title>Freeplay Solar Radio Brochure</dc:title>
<dc:date>1998-04-05</dc:date>
<dc:creator rdf:resource="#Tina"/>
<dc:language>en-US</dc:language>
<dc:format>application/pdf</dc:format>
<dc:description>The Freeplay(TM) Solar Radio never needs batteries -- the
  crank-up radio runs for an hour on a single crank up.  Solar power
  provides additional play time...</dc:description>
<dc:subject rdf:resource="&top;Marketing/Electronics/Audio"/>
<dc:coverage rdf:resource="#FreeplaySolarRadio"/>
</rdf:Description>

</rdf:RDF>
```

Figure 5.7: Sample metadata in RDF/XML

based on a simple taxonomy for browsing and navigation support and a (more complex) enterprise ontology to support semantic searching. The use of Semantic Web technologies within enterprise portals has been proposed in other research works such as OntoViews [MHSV04], ODESeW [CGPLC[+]03], and SEAL [SMS[+]01], the ideas have so far however not found their way into available products.

The use of semantic metadata promises a great improvement in searching (see chapters 7 and 8). It can be regarded as indispensable when trying to accomplish a proactive context-based information supply as motivated in chapter 2. However, the required manual creation of the metadata (also called annotation) remains as a major problem. Hence, the next chapter introduces an approach for a semi-automatic annotation of text documents based on text mining and information extraction techniques.

Chapter 6

Semi-automatic Annotation of Text Documents

This chapter sketches a semi-automatic approach for annotating text documents with semantic metadata based on text mining and information extraction techniques. The approach is a novel building block for the design presented in this work (*suggestion phase*). We suggest a to our knowledge unique hierarchical categorization for mapping documents into a taxonomy and a multi-label categorization for linking documents to elements from an ontology in section 6.3. Note however that the main contribution of this work is the context-based portlet integration presented in chapter 10. In order to integrate application portlets with unstructured documents managed by the content management service of an enterprise knowledge portal, we require an annotation of the documents with semantic metadata. The approach presented here should rather be seen as a byproduct of the above main proposal; its empirical evaluation is out of the scope of this work.

With the vision of the Semantic Web metadata has moved back into the center of attention. This manifests itself in standardization efforts and in a number of newer research works. Meanwhile a number of tools exists for metadata storage and querying (see chapter 4), a major problem is however the creation of the metadata. If a user checks a document into a knowledge or document management system, he/she has to manually define the relevant metadata. Users will, however, only be willing to perform this extra work, if they see a benefit from it. An improvement, e.g., in information retrieval, will however only be achieved if a certain critical mass of metadata-enriched documents is present in the system. This vicious circle is so far unsolved.

This chapter therefore identifies suitable text mining and information extraction techniques that can support the annotation of text documents with semantic metadata. Since metadata is only useful if a sufficient quality can be assured, fully automatic approaches for metadata creation are questionable. We propose a semi-automatic approach, i.e. the system should suggest automatically generated values to the user, allowing him/her, however, to correct them manually.

6.1 Text Mining and Information Extraction

Text mining deals with finding patterns and extracting knowledge from unstructured text documents. Since the older discipline data mining deals with the extraction of patterns from structured data, text mining can be seen as a special application field of data mining [Tan99]. Text mining also involves elements from a number of other areas, e.g., information retrieval (IR) [BYRN99], information extraction and machine learning.

In order to be able to apply classical data mining algorithms, the text documents must first be converted into a structured form. Tan [Tan99] calls this the text refining phase, which has a "document-based intermediate form" as result. The individual steps of the text preprocessing are:

- The tokenization step recognizes logical units of the text, i.e. separates it into words.

- Second, frequently occurring words without an individual meaning, so-called stopwords (e.g., "and", "is"), are eliminated.

- Stemming reduces inflection forms of a word to the stem form.

- The final step identifies multi-word groups and dissolves ambiguities (homonyms and synonyms).

After finishing the preprocessing steps the document is represented as a vector. This approach is also used in IR (see chapter 7). A t-dimensional space is defined, where t corresponds to the number of terms of the used vocabulary. Therefore the approach is also called the Vector Space Model (VSM). A document vector $d_j = (w_{1,j}, w_{2,j}, ..., w_{t,j})$ (for document j) consists of the occurrence or weighting of the individual vocabulary terms in the document [BYRN99]. In the simplest case, binary weightings can be used, i.e. $w_{i,j}$ is 1 if document j contains term i and 0 if not.

The weighted term frequency weights the individual terms by their number of occurrence in a document and the discrimination of the term with regard to the document collection. The weighting is computed as follows:

$$w_{i,j} = tf_{i,j} \times log\left(\frac{N}{df_i}\right)$$

The term frequency $tf_{i,j}$ stands for the number of occurrence of term i in document j, N for the number of documents in the document collection and the document frequency df_i for the number of documents, which contain the term i. Again, the result $w_{i,j}$ is the value of term i in the vector of document j; all vectors of the available document collection form a (weighted) term frequency matrix.

However, for any nontrivial document base, the number of terms t is usually quite large. Such high dimensionality leads to very sparse vectors and increases the difficulty in detecting and exploiting the relationships among terms. To overcome these problems, a *latent semantic indexing* method has been developed that effectively reduces the size of the vectors. It uses singular value decomposition (SVD), a well-known technique in matrix theory, to reduce the size of the term frequency matrix. Given a $t \times N$ term frequency matrix representing t terms and N documents, the SVD method removes rows and columns to reduce the matrix to size $K \times K$, where K is usually taken to be around a few hundred for large document collections. To minimize the information loss, only the least significant parts of the frequency matrix are omitted [BYRN99].

6.1.1 Automatic Text Categorization

Text categorization is the assignment of one or more predefined categories to a text document; examples are email spam filters (categories spam/non-spam) or a taxonomy-based categorization (see below). Formally, a Boolean value is assigned to each pair $< d_j, c_i > \in D \times C$, where D represents a set of documents and C a set of categories [Seb02]. We differentiate between single-label and multi-label categorization, according to whether exactly one or several categories are to be assigned to a document. If the documents are represented in the structured form of a document vector, well-known data mining classification algorithms can be applied for this purpose.

Classification is a supervised learning scheme that predicts the discrete class of an instance using a classifier, which is learned using a preclassified training data set [WF00], i.e. in this case a set of preclassified documents is required. Classification techniques can be directly applied for a single-label categorization (i.e. the classes correspond to the categories). For a multi-label categorization, multiple binary classifiers must be learned, one for each individual category. Each classifier decides whether a document is assigned to a certain category or not, i.e. each classifier only differentiates between true and false. Alternatively, the learning method may produce a likelihood of the category being assigned, and if, e.g., five categories were sought for the new document, the five with the highest likelihoods could be chosen. Typical classification algorithms are the following:

- *Decision trees* are created by recursively allocating the training data. There are different algorithms; one of the most well-known ones is ID3, which is also used within the C4.5 algorithm [Qui86]. A purely nominal evaluation is performed, which is why metric attributes first have to be discretized. Since the document vector contains solely metric attributes, this is a great disadvantage. Also the large number of attributes is an argument against the decision tree.

- In principle the *Naive Bayes* approach is more suitable for the classification of documents, since it can also easily consider numeric values, assuming that they are normally distributed. Naive Bayes determines the most probable class by means of conditioned probabilities. However it should be noted that for the classification of new documents a density function has to be computed for each class for each attribute.

- In *instance-based classification*, e.g., K-Nearest-Neighbor, no model is generated; instead the training data is stored and consulted for the classification of a new instance. The nearest neighbor of an instance is determined by the distance of its attribute values to other instances. K defines the number of neighbors that are considered. For the new instance the majority class of the K neighbors is selected. For text mining the cosine similarity, which is well-known from information retrieval [BYRN99], can be used as a distance measure (see also chapter 7). This approach is particularly suitable for text mining, since solely metric attributes are present and the computation is fast and simple.

- *Support Vector Machines* offer a further approach for the classification of text documents. It is based on the structural risk minimization principle [Vap95] of the computational learning theory. Linear limit functions are learned; the goal is to find a hyperplane in the document vector space, which divides it into two halves based on the class allocation. Hence, in their basic form Support Vector Machines allow only a binary classification. There are however a number of modifications, which allow the definition of several classes.

No general statements on the suitability or performance of certain classification algorithms are possible; it always depends on the data [MST94]. If one regards the characteristics of the data set (for text mining, e.g., the number of attributes is very large, however the number of instances relatively small), the number of potential classification approaches can be limited. In order to obtain an optimal performance, however, always several algorithms should be evaluated.

For the evaluation of classifiers their effectiveness is regarded, i.e. the ability to make a correct classification decision. Usually performance measures such as accuracy (fraction of the correctly classified instances) and the error rate (fraction of the wrongly classified instances) are consulted for the evaluation. For text (in particular multi-label) categorization however the precision and recall measures from information retrieval (see chapter 7) are also often used as decision criteria. In this context, precision indicates the fraction of the relevant categories within the found categories. The recall indicates the fraction of the relevant categories, which were found.

There were already numerous surveys on the suitability of classification algorithms for text mining. The data set that is usually taken for the evaluation is the Reuters 21578 corpus[1], consisting of reports from different economic areas. In a comparison of five benchmarks, Sebastiani [Seb02] comes to the conclusion that Naive Bayes and decision trees perform fairly bad. Support Vector Machines and the K-Nearest-Neighbor algorithm are among the winners.

6.1.2   Clustering of Documents

The goal of clustering is the allocation of input data into dynamically formed groups (clusters), such that the instances within a group are very similar and those within different groups are as different as possible [WF00]. Clustering is an unsupervised learning scheme, i.e. no classes are given in advance.

Clustering algorithms can be applied for text mining in order to divide documents into similar groups. This approach can be utilized, for example, for visualizing search results (presenting clusters of similar retrieved documents). Also interesting is the application of clustering for the creation of a taxonomy (see below), i.e. clusters of documents can be considered as representing potential taxonomy topics.

Clustering algorithms (e.g., K-Means) are – like instance-based classification algorithms – based on a similarity or distance function. Hence, measures like the cosine similarity can again be borrowed from information retrieval (see chapter 7).

6.1.3   Term-based Association Analysis

The association analysis identifies dependencies between attributes. Individual attributes or a combination of attributes can be predicted [WF00]. A classic example of an association analysis in data mining is a market basket analysis (i.e. finding products which are frequently bought together).

For text mining this means that words or terms are found, which frequently appear together in documents (e.g., dollars, shares, exchange, securities, etc.). Each document can be viewed as a transaction, while a set of terms in the document can be considered as a set of items in the transaction. For example, association mining can help detect synonyms and hypernyms in the preprocessing phase.

Usually more interesting than associations between arbitrary words are, however, associations between certain entities, like persons or company names (e.g., to detect potential mergers

---

[1]Available   at   http://www.daviddlewis.com/resources/testcollections/reuters-21578/ and http://kdd.ics.uci.edu/databases/reuters21578/reuters21578.html

and acquisitions). These "features" must then first be extracted by information extraction techniques (see below).

6.1.4 Information Extraction

Information extraction (IE) is a relatively young discipline. Text mining tries to find patterns in a number of text documents; information extraction aims at extracting certain text segments from single documents. While in classical text mining documents can be reduced to a set of words (i.e. a document vector), linguistic techniques, e.g., part-of-speech tagging (to recognize word types, i.e. nouns, verbs, etc.) and syntactic parsing (to recognize sentence structures, i.e. subject, predicate, object, etc.), have to be applied as a preprocessing step for information extraction.

The major (feasible) IE technique is *entity extraction*. An entity is an object, e.g., a person or an organization. Since such objects usually carry a name, which is to be extracted, the approach is also called named entity extraction. It can, for example, be used as a feature extraction step for an association analysis (see above) or for annotating documents if no controlled vocabulary (e.g., ontology) exists (see section 6.3.2). Today's extraction systems handle the extraction of (named) entities acceptably well. Scheffler et al. [SDW01], for example, present an approach based on hidden Markov models.

Besides entity extraction, approaches exist for extracting attributes of entities (other that its name, e.g., job position), facts (relations between entities, e.g., a person and the company he/she works for), and events (activities that involve one or more entities); their extraction quality is however still rather limited.

6.1.5 Automatic Text Summarization

A further area related to text mining and information extraction is automatic text summarization. The goal is to create a kind of abstract of the text, which contains all important information of the original document, however is substantially shorter. There are statistic and linguistic approaches.

Without going into details, *statistic approaches* are based on a structured representation of the documents, for example the Vector Space Model. One possible approach is the gradual search for expressive words on the basis of the weighted term frequency (see above). First the document is divided into sections (e.g., paragraphs or sentences). For each section the total weighted term frequency of all occurring words is determined. Those sections with the highest value are extracted as the text summary.

In *linguistic approaches* [BE97] not only the occurrence of individual terms in the document are considered, but also their meaning and interdependencies. Statistic approaches have the risk that semantically related sentences are torn apart and that the summary becomes incomprehensible. However, they are faster than linguistic approaches as these rely on complex preprocessing steps like the ones used for information extraction (see above).

6.2 Related Work

Meanwhile a number of commercial tools for text mining and information extraction is available. Prominent examples are the IDOL server of Autonomy[2] and AeroText[3] by Lockheed

---

[2]http://www.autonomy.com
[3]http://mds.external.lmco.com/products/gims/aero/

Martin. Most of the above techniques are supported: automatic text categorization, clustering, automatic text summarization, named entity extraction, etc. We base our implementation on the free JBowl[4] library, to which however a few extensions have to be made (see section 6.4).

There is a multiplicity of systems that have appeared on the market as knowledge, document and content management systems, as well as knowledge or enterprise portals. Livelink by OpenText[5], Hyperwave[6], and the SAP Enterprise Portal (see chapter 3) are only some few examples. These systems also use metadata for organizing the managed information and documents. Hence, an automatic or semi-automatic annotation is appropriate for them as well. In general, the automatic categorization of texts using a pre-defined taxonomy is supported by all mentioned products and can thus be seen as state-of-the-art. However, usually only relatively simple classifiers based on the Naive Bayes algorithm are available. Due to the unguaranteeable classification quality the applicability of the available mechanisms in practice is partially questionable, in particular as only few systems, e.g., Livelink, pursue a semi-automatic approach with control by the user.

In the scientific literature some work can be found on an automatic creation of ontologies [Mae02, PB03]. The use of text mining techniques for the semantic annotation of documents is however less regarded. Paralic & Bednar [PB03] give some however little concrete suggestions. Kao et al. [KQPW03] describe a semi-automatic approach for the classification of documents using a taxonomy. With S-CREAM, Handschuh et al. [HSC02] provide an approach for linking documents with elements from an ontology based on the information extraction system (see section 6.1.4) Amilcare[7].

6.3 Automatic Generation of Metadata Elements

In the following we discuss how the above text mining and information extraction techniques can be applied for automatically generating metadata elements. As mentioned in section 5.2 we base our analysis on the Dublin Core metadata set. In general, we propose a semi-automatic approach, i.e. the automatically generated values should be presented to the user as defaults that he/she can check and correct or complete where necessary.

For the metadata elements dc:title, dc:creator, dc:date, and dc:format simple heuristics seem more appropriate than complex text mining techniques. For example, the first line of a document can be used as the title, or layout characteristics, e.g., HTML tags, can be analyzed. The username and the date of creation can usually be queried from the operating system or the information is already included in the document in structured form, e.g., as Microsoft Office properties. The Dublin Core element dc:format, which specifies the media type (MIME type) of the document, can usually be recognized from the file extension or from information in the file header.

In order to be able to apply text mining techniques, the determination of the language of a document is required as a preprocessing step anyway. This can be achieved by comparing the words of the document with the vocabularies of different languages. For example, Grefenstette & Nioche [GN00] describe an approach which searches the document for frequent stop words of the individual languages.

The Dublin Core element dc:description specifies the extent of a resource in form of a table of contents or abstract, i.e. techniques for automatic text summarization (see section

---

[4]http://webocrat.fei.tuke.sk/jbowl/
[5]http://www.opentext.com
[6]http://www.hyperwave.com
[7]http://nlp.shef.ac.uk/amilcare/

6.1.5) can be applied. In particular statistic approaches should be appropriate, if the document is already represented by a document vector.

The values of dc:subject and dc:coverage use a controlled vocabulary, which can be, among other coding schemes, a taxonomy or an ontology. In the following we will therefore analyze the applicability of automatic text categorization techniques for this purpose.

6.3.1 Taxonomy-based Categorization

As already described in section 5.3, a taxonomy consists of a hierarchically ordered set of categories. An existing taxonomy can serve as a coding scheme for the Dublin Core element dc:subject, which determines the topic of a document. A taxonomy does not have to be provided completely manually. As mentioned above, the process of creating a taxonomy can be supported by clustering methods (see section 6.1.2).

For a taxonomy-based categorization of a text document automatic text categorization techniques can be utilized. Each element of the taxonomy represents a category. The taxonomy of a larger enterprise will probably consist of hundreds or thousands of categories. A document will however, as already explained, tendentiously only be assigned to one or very few categories. Hence, the use of a single-label categorization seems most appropriate. The corresponding classification problem has the following characteristics:

- Large number of (nominal) classes

- Large number of (metric) attributes

A classification based on the Naive Bayes algorithm is provided by many commercial systems (e.g., the SAP Enterprise Portal or LiveLink by OpenText). As shown in section 6.1.1, other algorithms – in particular instance-based approaches and extensions of Support Vector Machines that support multiple classes – promise however better classification results.

In addition, we propose to utilize the hierarchical structure of the taxonomy by applying a stepwise refining hierarchical classification [PKK05]. Instead of using each element of the taxonomy as a class, only the elements of a single hierarchy level are considered. The classification is done iteratively; when the suitable class (category) in a hierarchy level is found, its subcategories are used for a subsequent classification step. The classification along the taxonomy hierarchy is continued until a further degree of detail does no longer improve the confidence of the classification. Figure 6.1 shows an example of such a hierarchical classification. The dark grey elements represent the selected classes.

6.3.2 Linking Documents to Elements from an Ontology

The extent of a document (represented by the Dublin Core element dc:coverage) is determined by a set of objects or entities, which occur in the document text. If no catalog of possible objects exists (e.g., in form of an ontology), the extraction of entities by means of information extraction techniques (see section 6.1.4) can be applied. For this purpose a name recognizer needs to be provided that recognizes and extracts the appropriate terms in the regarded document. The approaches are based on natural language processing (NLP) techniques and thus very complex and error-prone.

It is therefore recommended to use an enterprise ontology as a controlled vocabulary for dc:coverage (see section 5.4). The creation of an ontology can also be achieved semi-automatically [Mae02]. For example, information extraction can be used to extract named entities (see sectan 6.1.4) and association analysis can uncover semantic connections between

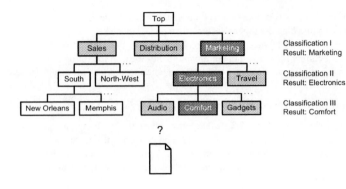

Classification I
Result: Marketing

Classification II
Result: Electronics

Classification III
Result: Comfort

Figure 6.1: Hierarchical taxonomy-based categorization

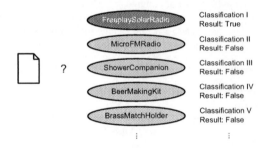

Classification I
Result: True

Classification II
Result: False

Classification III
Result: False

Classification IV
Result: False

Classification V
Result: False

Figure 6.2: Binary classifiers for linking a document with ontology elements

terms [PB03] (see section 6.1.3). In an enterprise context it is however often more practicable to provide an ontology from existing structured databases or a data warehouse which usually contains most objects that are relevant to the enterprise (products, departments, etc.).

With an ontology as a controlled vocabulary, the automatic linking of a document to related ontology elements is similar to a taxonomy-based categorization. However an ontology contains substantially more instances than a taxonomy, usually several thousands. A further characteristic of dc:coverage is that usually more than one element from the ontology can be assigned to a document. In this case it thus makes sense to use a multi-label categorization. The classification problem has the following characteristics:

- Dichotomy (true/false) as classes

- Large number of (metric) attributes

- Instances are very unequally distributed (most instances do *not* contain a certain element).

As stated in section 6.1.1, a binary classifier must be learned for each individual category. Each classifier decides whether a document contains a certain element or not. Afterwards the positively classified elements are used as values for dc:coverage. This clasification process is depicted in figure 6.2.

From the approaches presented in section 6.1.1 the Support Vector Machines are particularly suitable for a binary classification. Additionally the binary logistic regression and the discriminant analysis can be applied. These are statistic approaches, which similarly to the support vector machines try to divide the two classes by means of a hyperplane. Fisher's linear discriminant analysis optimizes a square cost function; during the logistic regression the likelihood is maximized. Since the discriminant works with nominal, the logistic regression however with metric attributes, the binary logistic regression is more appropriate for text mining. It has also scored very well in many classification comparisons [KB04, MST94].

6.4 Summary

We have examined text mining and information extraction for their suitability for creating semantic metadata for text documents. Based on the Dublin Core metadata standard [DCM03] we have identified techniques for various metadata elements. These are being integrated as a semi-automatic approach into the INWISS knowledge portal prototype[8]. The prototype covered in chapter 11; a proposal for a content management service (and corresponding portlet) is sketched in section 11.5.

To our knowledge, the suggested gradually proceeding hierarchical classification for mapping documents into a taxonomy is particularly new. This approach promises a clear improvement of the classification quality; the evaluation is however subject to future work. Also new is the linking of the documents to elements from an ontology. For this purpose we propose a multi-label categorization based on binary classifiers.

For the taxonomy-based categorization we have proposed a single-label approach. However, a multi-label categorization should also be considered as an alternative. While the single-label approach will achieve a better precision with the cost of missing potential additional categories, multiple binary classifiers will achieve a better recall (finding all relevant categories) with the cost of a worse precision (i.e. including also irrelevant ones). It can be argued that for a semi-automatic approach recall is more important than precision; this however needs to be evaluated empirically.

As already mentioned, our implementation is based on the Java Text Mining and Retrieval Library (formerly known as Java Bag of Words Library) JBowl[9]. For a first empirical evaluation we use the already mentioned Reuters 21578 text corpus, in which 21,578 annotated documents are available as a training and test set. The documents are assigned to topics (comparably with a taxonomy) and contain references to companies, organizations, persons and places that occur in the text (comparable with an ontology). A newer version of the corpus uses a hierarchical taxonomy such that an evaluation of our hierarchical categorization approach can be pursued.

As future work, we are extending our metadata-based search engine (see chapter 8 and section 11.4) with fulltext search capabilities. This new version is based on the Jakarta Lucene information retrieval framework[10]. An extension of JBowl and the integration with Lucene is the subject of a joint project with the research group working on JBowl in Kosice, Slovakia[11].

---

[8]http://www.inwiss.org

[9]http://webocrat.fei.tuke.sk/jbowl/

[10]http://jakarta.apache.org/lucene/

[11]The work is partly funded as a bilateral project by the German Academic Exchange Service (DAAD) and the Slovak Ministry of Education (grant no. D/04/25716).

Chapter 7

Global Searching

As elaborated in chapter 3, a major requirement for an enterprise knowledge portal is to be able to globally search for information, no matter where this information is stored or which piece of software manages it. The system should find articles from the content management component of the portal or an external content management system, documents from a document management system, reports from a business intelligence system, etc. As part of the *suggestion phase* of the research effort presented in this work, this chapter covers state-of-practice building blocks of the proposed design in the area of information retrieval (IR), in particular techniques for repository integration and meta searching. Using semantic (ontology-based) metadata for searching requires an adaption of existing IR techniques; a novel similarity-based approach is presented in the next chapter.

Large amounts of information in today's enterprises exist as unstructured documents. The challenge is to make these documents available to the user. Search engines are used to provide the user with documents that are "relevant" for his information need (see chapter 2). The research discipline addressing this issue is called *information retrieval (IR)* [BYRN99]. This chapter presents an overview of information retrieval techniques that can be applied in enterprise knowledge portals. Classic information retrieval systems search text documents for keywords provided by a user query. Web search engines like Google[1] are the most prominent examples for IR on a huge document base (in this case more or less the whole accessible Internet). Throughout this chapter we will particularly comment on the applicability of the presented approaches also for metadata-based searches as proposed in chapter 5.

One of the differences between the retrieval in databases (also called data or fact retrieval) and information retrieval is that data retrieval works on strongly structured data records while information retrieval usually deals with unstructured texts. This difference has already been discussed in the context of data and text mining in chapter 6. The main difference lies, however, in the fuzziness of the queries. Data retrieval queries are exact and deterministic while information retrieval queries are fuzzy and try to find relevant items based on a best-match paradigm.

Van Rijsbergen [vR79] summarizes the differences between data and information retrieval as shown in table 7.1:

- Data retrieval (DR) is normally looking for an *exact match*, i.e. checking to see whether an item is or is not present in the database. Information retrieval (IR) tries to find those items

---

[1]`http://www.google.com`

Table 7.1: Information retrieval vs. data retrieval [vR79]

	Data Retrieval (DR)	Information Retrieval (IR)
Matching	Exact match	Partial match, best match
Inference	Deduction	Induction
Model	Deterministic	Probabilistic
Classification	Monothetic	Polythetic
Query language	Artificial	Natural
Query specification	Complete	Incomplete
Items wanted	Matching	Relevant
Error response	Sensitive	Insensitive

which *partially match* the request and then select from those a few of the *best matching* ones.

- The inference used in DR is of a simple *deductive* kind, i.e. if $a \rightarrow b$ and $b \rightarrow c$ then $a \rightarrow c$. In IR it is far more common to use *inductive* inference; relations are only specified with a degree of certainty or uncertainty and hence the confidence in the inference is variable.

- The above distinction leads to describing data retrieval as *deterministic* but information retrieval as *probabilistic*.

- Another distinction can be made in terms of classifications that are likely to be useful. DR most likely uses a *monothetic* classification, i.e. classes are defined by objects possessing attributes both necessary and sufficient for belonging to a class. In IR more often a *polythetic* classification is desired, i.e. each individual in a class will possess only a proportion of the attributes possessed by the members of the class; no attribute is necessary nor sufficient.

- The query language for DR will generally be of an *artificial* kind with restricted syntax and vocabulary, in IR it is preferred to use *natural* language although there are some exceptions.

- In DR the query is generally a *complete* specification of what is wanted, in IR it is invariably *incomplete*.

- The last difference arises partly from the fact that in IR we are searching for *relevant* documents as opposed to exactly *matching* items. The extent of the match in IR is assumed to indicate the likelihood of the relevance of that item.

- As a consequence of the previous difference, DR is more *sensitive* to error in the sense that, an error in matching will not retrieve the wanted item which implies a total failure of the system. In IR small errors in matching generally do not affect performance of the system significantly.

Lately, however, an increasing convergence of the two areas can be observed [Fer03]. Databases try more and more to deal also with textual data (e.g. by integrating fulltext search capabilities) while information retrieval more and more tries to also consider the text structure and document metadata.

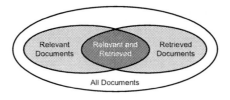

Figure 7.1: Relevant vs. retrieved documents

7.1 Evaluation of Information Retrieval Systems

Numerous criteria for the evaluation of information retrieval systems have been proposed in the literature. The primary goal of a retrieval system is to find as many relevant and as little irrelevant documents with regard to a certain user query [BYRN99]. This first leads to the question what "relevance" actually means.

> Cuadra & Katter [CK67] define relevance as "the correspondence in context between an information requirement statement (a query) and an article (a document), that is, the extent to which the article covers the material that is appropriate to the requirement statement."

However, this definition now opens up the question what "correspondence in context" and "appropriate" are supposed to mean. In fact, in practice the only way to judge about relevance is to use the intuitive or naive meaning of the term used by humans. The evaluation of information retrieval systems hence aims at determining in how far the system obtains the same results as test persons, i.e. how well they simulate human behavior.

Based on the notion of relevance, usually tested empirically, the two most important performance measures for information retrieval systems are recall and precision. The *recall* is defined as the number of retrieved relevant documents relative to the number of all relevant documents (see figure 7.1); it can take values between 0 and 1 with 1 being an ideal value meaning that all relevant documents were found:

$$recall = \frac{|relevant\ documents \cap retrieved\ documents|}{|relevant\ documents|}$$

Likewise, the *precision* is the quotient of the number of retrieved relevant documents and the number of all retrieved documents. It indicates which proportion of the found documents is actually relevant:

$$precision = \frac{|relevant\ documents \cap retrieved\ documents|}{|retrieved\ documents|}$$

Like the recall, the precision can take values between 0 and 1 with an ideal case of 1 meaning that all found documents are relevant, i.e. no useless documents were included in the query result.

In some way the two measures recall and precsion are moving in opposite directions. This becomes evident when regarding the two extreme cases: If all existing documents are returned as the result of a query, the recall is equal to 1. The precision will however be very bad (if not all documents are relevant). In reverse if only one relevant document is found, then the precision is equal to 1 and the recall will be very bad (if there is more than one relevant document in the document base). Usually the result will however be between these two extremes. In general reducing the result set through a more specific query leads to a better precision but a worse recall; enlarging the result set through a more general query leads to a larger recall but a smaller precision [Fer03].

The contrary direction of the two measures becomes particularly evident for systems which provide rank orders of documents as result sets such as the Vector Space Model (see next section). With such rank orders it is possible to show the connection between precision and recall by specifying a similarity threshold in such a way that the desired result set is obtained. A so-called precision recall diagram can be created by counting the relevant and irrelevant documents – step by step following the rank order of the result set – and by computing a new precision recall pair for every new relevant document found.

In addition to recall and precision, Cleverdon et al. [CMK66] propose four additional criteria for evaluating information retrieval systems:

- The *time lag* is the average time between the start of a query and the delivery of the results [CMK66]. Obviously, the goal is to minimize the time lag. It is, however, affected by many variables (e.g. size of database, database system used, hardware, etc.) and is in conflict with other quality criteria.

- The *effort* denotes the intellectual and physical effort, a user must put into receiving an answer to his query from the information retrieval system [CMK66]. The system should be usable in an intuitive way. For example, for a Boolean retrieval a simple standard search should be offered, in which the search terms are automatically combined with a logical AND (see section 7.2); an advanced search should provide various user-defined settings (e.g. the use of a logical OR).

- The *form of presentation* describes the way the result is presented to the user [CMK66]. Different presentation forms should be offered, e.g. the choice to decide in which order the documents of the result set are returned (descending relevance, descending date of preparation, etc.). Besides, it should be possible to select which information on the documents is displayed (e.g. only author, title, and date of preparation, or also a summary of the document).

- The *coverage of the collection* is the degree, to which relevant documents are stored in the system [CMK66]. Information retrieval is however only part of the overall knowledge management process; it must be "fed" by other subprocesses (see chapter 2). The coverage of the collection is rather an evaluation criterion for these knowledge creating processes than for the retrieval.

7.2   Classic Information Retrieval Models

Information retrieval (IR) systems can be based on various different so-called retrieval models. Figure 7.2 gives an overview of those models. The most well-known ones are the Boolean retrieval model and the Vector Space Model. In the figure structured retrieval and browsing models are shown apart from these classical models that we will discuss below in more detail. In structured models also the structure of the documents is considered besides the content. Browsing models deal with (e.g. taxonomy-based) navigation through a document base, rather than answering search queries [BYRN99].

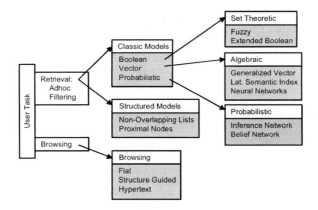

Figure 7.2: Classification of information retrieval models [BYRN99]

7.2.1 Boolean Retrieval

Boolean retrieval is still frequently used in many commercial IR systems. It essentially breaks searching down to examining whether a well-defined condition, usually the occurence of a keyword in a text, holds or not. As a query result, it provides an unordered set of documents. Hence, according to the characteristics discussed above, Boolean retrieval systems follow rather a data or fact than an information retrieval approach; they perform an exact match and allow no ranking by relevance [Fer03].

The basic idea of Boolean retrieval is to apply set operations to sets of documents which are characterized by attribute values. An attribute is a relation, which assigns a value to a document. The basic element of a Boolean query is a pair of an attribute and a corresponding attribute value. Documents, for which the attribute takes the indicated value, satisfy this elementary query. For text documents the most important attributes are the occurrence of words (or terms) in the fulltext. Documents can however also be divided into different fields, i.e. an attribute may also indicate the occurence of a term in a certain field. This makes the approach easily applicable for metadata with different metadata elements or properties (e.g., dc:title, dc:creator). In fact, most Semantic Web query languages (e.g., RQL, RDQL) follow a Boolean-retrieval-like approach (see chapter 4).

7.2.2 Vector Space Model

The Vector Space Model (VSM) was already mentioned in the context of text mining in section 6.1. Both, the query and the documents are modeled as a vector using the same attribute space. The relevance ranking of a document with respect to a query depends on the distance of its vector to the query vector. Various distance measures have been proposed in the literature, experiments have shown that the so-called cosine similarity (based on the cosine of the angle defined by the query and document vectors) tends to lead to better results than most other measures (e.g., the Euclidean distance) [BYRN99].

Figure 7.3 shows the similarity ranking of two documents d_1 and d_2 with respect to query q. Note that the first document d_1 is "closer" to the query q when the distance is defined as the angle between the corresponding vectors. The second document d_2 ist "closer" to the query q

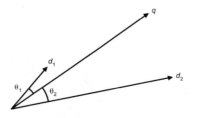

Figure 7.3: Similarity of two document vectors with respect to a query vector

when the distance is measured using the Euclidean norm. That is, $cos(\theta_1) < cos(\theta_2)$, while $|d_1 - q| > |d_2 - q|$.

As defined in section 6.1, $d_j = (w_{1,j}, w_{2,j}, ..., w_{t,j})$ corresponds to the document vector with weighting factors $w_{i,j}$ like the weighted term frequency (with term frequency $tf_{i,j}$ of term i in document j, the number of documents N, and the document frequency df_i of of term i):

$$w_{i,j} = tf_{i,j} \times log\left(\frac{N}{df_i}\right)$$

If $q = (w_{1,q}, w_{2,q}, ..., w_{t,q})$ represents the query vector correspondingly, the cosine similarity between document d_j and the query q is defined as follows:

$$sim(d_j, q) = \frac{d_j \cdot q}{|d_j| \cdot |q|} = \frac{\sum_{i=1}^{t} w_{i,j} \cdot w_{i,q}}{\sqrt{\sum_{i=1}^{t} w_{i,j}^2} \times \sqrt{\sum_{i=1}^{t} w_{i,q}^2}}$$

The model follows a fuzzy approach as also documents are found which only contain a subset of the query terms, and provides a ranked list of results sorted by a relevance score. A theoretical disadvantage is the assumption that the index terms are independent from each other, which is generally wrong. Nevertheless, the VSM is simple, fast, and performs at least as good as other known models; it is therefore very popular and also used by Google and most other Web search engines.

A fuzzy search approch like provided by the Vector Space Model is also desireble for metadata-based searches. The VSM is however optimized for being used with documents that are represented as vectors with term frequencies. Hence, in its original form it is only partly applicable for metadata. An adaption of the VSM for ontology-based semantic metadata will be presented in the next chapter.

7.3 Repository Integration and Indexing

The most straight-forward approach for providing a global search facility in enterprise knowl-edge portals is to integrate the individual data sources by providing a (possibly virtual) inte-grated repository. This way a search engine can search for resources from multiple sources without the need for collating multiple search results. The architecture for a global search through repository integration is shown in figure 7.4. The integration can either be achieved by making sure the different systems all use a centralized repository or by replicating the data from proprietary local repositories to a global one. In the latter case the replication is typically performed offline in a batch process.

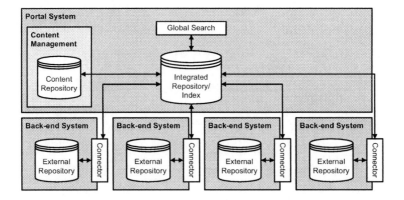

Figure 7.4: Global searching through repository integration

In principle it is possible to sequentially search the text documents without any preprocessing. Such a search is called on-line search and should be used only if the document base is relatively small and if very frequent changes (at least several times a day) occur. In order to accelerate the search, it is however advisable to create indexes [BYRN99]. An index-based search is appropriate for a large database that is less frequently updated. Usually a special representation of the resources is required that is more suitable for retrieval than the resources themselves (e.g. document vectors). This conversion can take place along with the indexing, together with other preprocessing steps that have already been discussed in the context of text mining in section 6.1 (stopword elimination, stemming, etc.).

On the Internet, search engines use so-called crawlers or spiders to locate webpages to be indexed, crawling the WWW by following hyperlinks. In an enterprise environment connectors to different source systems can be used. For example, the SAP Enterprise Portal (see chapter 3) uses so-called Repository Managers (RM) for accessing external data sources trough the Repository Framework (RF) [SAP03]. A Repository Manager is responsible for converting the repository's internal representation of the stored information into the unified aspects of the RF and vice versa. When the RF is extended with a new repository, all objects exposed by this new repository can instantly be searched using the generic TREX search engine without the need for re-implementing such functionality in the repository itself. The TREX indexing mechanism indexes resources from all repositories by extracting their content through the RF. There are currently various Repository Managers available for a number of existing content and document management systems, e.g. Lotus Notes/Domino or the IBM DB2 Content Manager.

As already mentioned in chapter 5 it is a common approach to use metadata for searching, rather than (only) terms that occur in the fulltext. We argue that this search approach also allows semantic searches, e.g. for resources dealing with a certain product, particularly if an enterprise ontology is used as a controlled vocabulary.

In this case, repository integration also means metadata integration. The ideal situation would obviously be to have a single enterprise-wide metadata repository that is used by all system components. However, due to the independence of (standard) software components that are being used, this is a difficult issue. The main problem is the heterogeneity of the metadata models, i.e. the metadata elements used to describe resources and their value domains. Standardization efforts like the Dublin Core Metadata Initiative presented in chapter 5 try to

```
@prefix rdf: <http://www.w3.org/1999/02/22-rdf-syntax-ns#> .
@prefix rdfs: <http://www.w3.org/2000/01/rdf-schema#> .
@prefix owl: <http://www.w3.org/2002/07/owl#> .
@prefix dc: <http://purl.org/dc/elements/1.1/> .
@prefix : <http://www.inwiss.org/ontology#> .


<http://www.microstrategy.com/terms/name> owl:equivalentProperty dc:title .
<http://www.microstrategy.com/terms/owner> owl:equivalentProperty
  dc:creator .
<http://www.microstrategy.com/terms/modified> owl:equivalentProperty
  dc:date .
<http://www.microstrategy.com/terms/folder> owl:equivalentProperty
  dc:subject .
<http://www.microstrategy.com/terms/element> owl:equivalentProperty
  dc:coverage .

<http://www.microstrategy.com/elements/Item_83> owl:sameAs
  :FreeplaySolarRadio .
<http://www.microstrategy.com/elements/Item_131> owl:sameAs :MicroFMRadio .
<http://www.microstrategy.com/elements/Item_172> owl:sameAs
  :ShowerCompanion .
<http://www.microstrategy.com/elements/Item_15> owl:sameAs :BeerMakingKit .
<http://www.microstrategy.com/elements/Item_24> owl:sameAs
  :BrassMatchHolder .
...
```

Figure 7.5: Sample ontological mapping for metadata integration

develop standard metadata models; however it is not very likely that all software vendors will support a single common model in near future.

Luckily, the Semantic Web also has an answer to such heterogeneity issues (see chapter 4). Ontology languages like OWL [W3C04a] provide constructs for ontological mapping (synonyms, subclassing, etc.). This way, the individual systems can store their metadata using their own "language". Figure 7.5 shows an example in RDF/N3 how ontological mapping can help with mapping concepts of different metadata models. In our scenario, metadata of OLAP reports from the business intelligence (BI) system is represented by the metadata elements name, owner, modified, folder, and element; the content management service, however, uses Dublin Core. These can be mapped by using the owl:equivalentProperty directive.

If a controlled vocabulary (e.g., ontology) is used as metadata values, ontological mapping can also be applied to those vocabulary terms (ontology elements). In our scenario, the BI system uses numeric IDs to identify the individual elements (e.g., products) in a report. These can be mapped to their counterparts in the enterprise ontology by means of the owl:sameAs directive (as also shown in figure 7.5). Note, however, that searching for such ontology elements requires an adaption of the information retrieval techniques used. A similarity-based information retrieval approach for ontology-based metadata (inspired by IR models like the Vector Space Model) is presented in chapter 8.

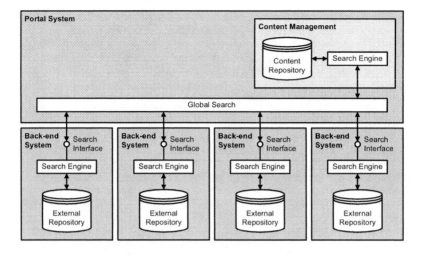

Figure 7.6: Global searching through meta searching

7.4 Meta Searching

Meta search engines are systems, which send a query to different search engines, combine the returned results, and present them altogether to the user [Fer03]. In other words, meta searching assumes that each individual system managing data from a certain source has its own search capabilities. The problem of providing a global search is to integrate these individual search mechanisms. A search user interface communicates with a global (so-called meta) search engine rather than a search engine for a particular data source. This meta search engine forwards the user's search request to the individual search engines and consolidates the search results. Figure 7.6 shows the architecture of such a meta search system.

Again, we find a counterpart on the Internet. Meta search engines like MetaCrawler[2] [SE97] forward searches to multiple Web search engines such as Google and Yahoo!, consolidate the results, and present them to the user as a single ranked result list.

Two main problems need to be addressed: Since the different search engines use different methods, they usually also use different formats and strategies for formulating queries. Such differences can exist on all levels of the question construction, beginning with the metadata elements and their vocabularies or classifications, up to different search methods like Boolean retrieval or VSM-based ranking. Again, the heterogeneity of the metadata models used by the different systems can be addressed by ontological mapping (e.g., the property dc:description might have to be mapped to livelink:abstract for a specific local search engine).

The second challenge is the organization and presentation of the returned results in a uniform way. Different degrees of integration are possible. The simplest way is to independently list the results of the individual search engines. It gets more complicated if the results are to be combined to a single ranked result list. The individual search engines all return their search results ranked by a score or match value. However, the scores of different search engines are usually not comparable, even if they use the same ranking algorithm [MYL02]. Hence, the

---

[2]http://www.metacrawler.com

challenge is the collation of these multiple different local rankings. MetaCrawler, for example, follows a very straight-forward approach by normalizing the individual scores into a range of 0 to 1,000. Thus, the top pick from each search engine will have a score of 1,000 [SE97]. More sophisticated approaches use statistics about the individual search engines to estimate their usefulness for a specific query, giving potentially more useful ones more weight in the global ranking [MYL02].

7.5 Summary

This chapter gave an overview on information retrieval techniques, in particular the Vector Space Model (VSM). Approaches for providing a global search facility in enterprise knowledge portals through repository integration and meta searching have been presented. Finally, the applicability of the presented approaches for metadata-based searches and the use of ontological mapping for overcoming heterogeneity issues of different information sources have been discussed.

Semantic Web technologies have so far however not found their way into today's systems. Most systems use free text or simple classification hierarchies as metadata values. This poses particular limitations on capabilities for context-based searching (as motivated in chapter 2). In order to be able to find documents that are related to other documents (or to a dynamically created user context), rich semantic links are required in the metadata. In chapter 5 we have proposed the use of an ontology for this purpose.

As already mentioned above, searches on ontology-based metadata require a fuzzy information retrieval approach which utilizes the semantic links of the ontology. Today's metadata querying approaches however do not provide such fuzziness. Hence, we propose a similarity-based approach inspired by information retrieval models like the Vector Space Model in the next chapter. This approach is implemented as part of our INWISS knowledge portal prototype[3] (see chapter 11). For global searching we follow a repository integration approach; web articles, external documents, and business intelligence reports are all represented by metadata in a central RDF repository.

---

[3]http://www.inwiss.org

Chapter 8

Similarity-based Information Retrieval on Metadata

This chapter introduces a similarity-based information retrieval approach for semantic (ontology-based) metadata. This is a again a *suggestion* for a novel building block of the IS design presented in this work. Again, the main contribution is the context-based portlet integration in chapter 10, which allows to use the context of an application portlet (viewing structured information) as a query to search for related unstructured information in form of documents. For this purpose, we require an approach for searching on semantic metadata rather than fulltext. However, like the approach for semi-automatic annotation in chapter 6, also the proposed information retrieval approach should rather be seen as a byproduct, required for evaluating the portlet integration.

Metadata has been used for searching by document and knowledge management systems for decades. The standard approach for searching metadata is to perform an exact query based on a Boolean search constraint specified by the user (e.g., `dc:title` = "x" AND `dc:creator` = "y"). This is also what current Semantic Web tools do for querying. There is no fuzziness or ranking as known from information retrieval models like the Vector Space Model (VSM). However, we argue that a fuzzy ranking is also needed for metadata searching. First, the metadata quality depends on the users' tagging, which is a voluntary process (that creates extra work). Second, a metadata model (and a corresponding ontology) can be expected to become quite complex. It is thus hard for users to build search queries that "perfectly" represent their information need.

In work on fuzzy (or vague) queries in structured databases Küng & Palkoska [KP97] distinguish the following four levels of fuzziness:

- *Crisp Data, Crisp Query, Crisp Result (CDCQ-CR):* An example would be a SQL query on a relational database, but also RDQL or RQL queries on an RDF repository, the current state-of-the art on the Semantic Web.

- *Crisp Data, Fuzzy Query, Fuzzy Result (CDFQ-FR):* By extending a SQL query with a fuzzy WHERE clause (e.g., by using the LIKE keyword and wildcards on strings) some means for this fuzziness level are provided in relational databases. For example, Sesame[1] [BKvH02] supports the same for string literals in its SeRQL query language for RDF.

---

[1] `http://www.openrdf.org`

- *Fuzzy Data, Fuzzy Query, Fuzzy Result (FDFQ-FR):* This fuzziness level deals with fuzzy data. There are some approaches in the database field using data ranges und multiple values for certain attributes. However, the basic idea of the Semantic Web is that there is no uncertainty in the data.

- *Crisp Data, Crisp Query, Fuzzy Result (CDCQ-FR):* The idea of this fuzziness level is that even though crisp data is stored in the database and the query is specified by concrete search values, the results should be fuzzy.

Our goal is to provide CDCQ-FR for semantic metadata. Crisp data is stored in the metadata repository, crisp queries are given searching for concrete metadata values, but the query results should be fuzzy and ranked by relevance. This is exactly what information retrieval (e.g., based on the VSM) does for fulltext, as a query for a number of keywords will also retrieve documents that only contain a subset of these keywords, however with a lower ranking.

8.1 Related Work

One of the great potentials of the Semantic Web is to provide better search engines that use semantic metadata queries rather than just keywords (see chapter 4). However, so far only few research results are available that try to bridge metadata technology from the Semantic Web with information retrieval research.

A quite complex framework that tries to bring these two fields together is OWLIR (Web Ontology Language and Information Retrieval) [SFJ+02]. The framework is used as a news repository and manages indexing of information, user querying, and qualifying of the results. It consists of various tools including third party software like AeroText[2], which automatically analyzes the documents and annotates them with metadata. At query time the system enriches the documents by information from an ontology using this metadata. The enriched document base is then searched via HAIRCUT [MMP99] by means of traditional information retrieval mechanisms. This combination of a distinctive knowledge base with IR techniques raises the precision of the results significantly; at least as far as the running prototype is concerned.

Where the OWLIR framework tries to use semantic information in the environment of traditional full-text retrieval, Stojanovic [Sto03] addresses the issue from another point of view. As the Semantic Web usually delivers exact results that are machine understandable the list of these results will be considerably different from the answers listed by classic search engines like Google. Where Google gives a list of ranked results there are only exact matches resulting from a query in the Semantic Web. However, even among the (exact) hits of a query it might be the case that some of the results found are more relevant to the users query than others. Considering a large database this could be a drawback in usability. Users are used to ranked lists and trust the system to deliver the really relevant documents among the top ten.

To enable ranking in a Semantic Web environment Stojanovic uses "ranking based on background information" on a part of the Semantic Web that was originally designed for something different: the proof layer (see chapter 4). In this layer agents are expected to record the path they took to infer the results. The outcome of a successful search should produce a kind of a tree. How relevant a result is can be measured by the path that was used to reach the result. If the tree for the result has many nodes with an AND connection – compared to an OR connection – the relevance of the path rises as the way through an AND node is more significant then through an OR node.

---

[2]http://mds.external.lmco.com/products/gims/aero/

Second, Stojanovic uses the size of the knowledge base, particularly the number of possible interpretations of a given instance. For example, if a query that searches for employees with knowledge about the Semantic Web delivers an instance that works in 3 projects, one having to do with the Semantic Web, it receives an ambiguity of 3, where an instance working only in the Semantic Web project receives an ambiguity value of 1. For the computation of the relevance the reciprocal – the specificity – is used. The model is implemented within the SEAL prototype [SMS+01]. For the initial semantic query OntoBroker [DEFS99] is utilized. Stojanovic [Sto03] presents a first approach to apply ranking to metadata-based Semantic Web searches. However, it still deals with exact queries. As mentioned above our goal is a search facility that supports fuzzy or vague queries on metadata.

8.2 Utilizing Ontology-based Metadata

Translating the similarity-based approach of IR models like the Vector Space Model to the world of semantic metadata means that we represent both the resources and queries as metadata descriptions and use their similarity for the ranking. As a user defines his query by constraining certain metadata properties, this set of properties can be represented as an RDF description. The query RDF description can possibly be anonymous, i.e. does not have to be identified by a URI, but can rather represented as a blank node [W3C04d].

Consider the sample metadata shown in figure 8.1 in RDF/N3 notation (see chapter 4). Four documents are given: a product brochure on the Freeplay Solar Radio product (a simplified version of the metadata description given in Figure 5.6 on page 62), an intranet news article on the opening of a new call center, and two business intelligence reports with sales numbers of the products of the Audio subcategory, respective the subcategories of the Electronics category (Resource4 corresponds to the report shown in figure 10.3 on page 111). In addition, four sample queries are provided and also represented in RDF: one searching for documents dealing with the Freeplay Solar Radio product, one searching for documents created by the employee Calvin. Query3 and Query4 are assumed to be implicit queries trying to find resources that are related to the resources Resource3 and Resource4. They represent the context of OLAP reports [CD97] provided by a reporting portlet (see chapter 10).

In addition to the metadata, consider the excerpt of the OWL ontology shown in Figure 8.2. It shows that Tina works in the headquarters in New York, that New York belongs to the North-East region, and that the Freeplay Solar Radio, Micro FM Radio, and Shower Companion products all belong to the Audio subcategory which itself belongs to the Electronics category. The full ontology of our scenario (without instances) is shown as a UML diagram in appendix A.1. Linking this ontology to the resource metadata from Figure 8.1 leads to a graph structure. The metadata of Resource1 is represented by the RDF graph shown in figure 8.3.

The idea for a fuzzy similarity-based retrieval now is to find also distant (indirect) links. A query for the Freeplay Solar Radio product should also find resources dealing with the Audio subcategory or other products belonging to it. On first sight this leads to the necessity to apply graph matching techniques computing the similarity of RDF graphs. This has been shown by Carrol [Car02] to be very complex and rather unsuitable for efficient searching.

As elaborated in chapter 4, the logic layer of the Semantic Web provides means for inferring implicit information in a way that makes it explicit for querying applications. In OWL properties can be defined to be transitive (by defining them as an owl:TransitiveProperty) such that a resource A that is linked to B which itself is linked to C is implicitly also linked to C. Inference engines can automatically generate such implicit RDF triples and add them to the repository.

```
@prefix dc:   <http://purl.org/dc/elements/1.1/> .
@prefix onto: <http://www.inwiss.org/ontology#> .
@prefix :     <http://www.inwiss.org/samples/> .

# Sample resources
:Resource1 dc:title "Freeplay Solar Radio Brochure" .
:Resource1 dc:creator onto:Tina .
:Resource1 dc:coverage onto:FreeplaySolarRadio .

:Resource2 dc:title "New Calling Center opened in Atlanta, GA" .
:Resource2 dc:creator onto:Calvin .
:Resource2 dc:coverage onto:CC_Atlanta .

:Resource3 dc:title "Audio Sales 1998"
:Resource3 dc:creator onto:Ted .
:Resource3 dc:coverage onto:FreeplaySolarRadio .
:Resource3 dc:coverage onto:MicroFMRadio .
:Resource3 dc:coverage onto:ShowerCompanion .

:Resource4 dc:title "Electronics Sales 1998"
:Resource4 dc:creator onto:Ted .
:Resource4 dc:coverage onto:Audio .
:Resource4 dc:coverage onto:Comfort .
:Resource4 dc:coverage onto:Gadgets .

# Sample queries
:Query1 dc:coverage onto:FreeplaySolarRadio .

:Query2 dc:creator onto:Calvin .

:Query3 dc:coverage onto:FreeplaySolarRadio .
:Query3 dc:coverage onto:MicroFMRadio .
:Query3 dc:coverage onto:ShowerCompanion .

:Query4 dc:coverage onto:Audio .
:Query4 dc:coverage onto:Comfort .
:Query4 dc:coverage onto:Gadgets .
```

Figure 8.1: Sample metadata in N3 notation

```
@prefix rdf:  <http://www.w3.org/1999/02/22-rdf-syntax-ns#>
@prefix :  <http://www.inwiss.org/ontology#>

:Calvin rdf:type :Manager .
:Calvin :office :CC_Atlanta .
:Calvin :division :Sales .

:Tina rdf:type :Employee .
:Tina :office :Headquarters .
:Tina :division :Marketing .

:Ted rdf:type :Employee .
:Ted :office :Headquarters .
:Ted :division :Finance .

:CC_Atlanta rdf:type :CallCenter .
:CC_Atlanta :city :Atlanta .

:Headquarters rdf:type :Office .
:Headquarters :city :NewYork .

:Atlanta rdf:type :City .
:Atlanta :region :SouthEast .

:NewYork rdf:type :City .
:NewYork :region :NorthEast .

:FreeplaySolarRadio rdf:type :Item .
:FreeplaySolarRadio :subcategory :Audio .

:MicroFMRadio rdf:type :Item .
:MicroFMRadio :subcategory :Audio .

:ShowerCompanion rdf:type :Item .
:ShowerCompanion :subcategory :Audio .

:Audio rdf:type :Subcategory .
:Audio :category :Electronics .

...
```

Figure 8.2: Excerpt of the ontology

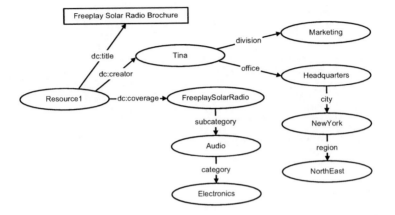

Figure 8.3: Sample metadata as RDF graph

```
@prefix dc:    <http://purl.org/dc/elements/1.1/>
@prefix onto:  <http://www.inwiss.org/ontology#>
@prefix :      <http://www.inwiss.org/samples/>

:Resource1 dc:title "Freeplay Solar Radio Brochure" .
:Resource1 dc:creator onto:Tina .
:Resource1 dc:creator onto:Marketing .
:Resource1 dc:creator onto:Headquarters .
:Resource1 dc:coverage onto:FreeplaySolarRadio .
:Resource1 dc:coverage onto:Audio .
:Resource1 dc:coverage onto:Electronics .

:Query1 dc:coverage onto:FreeplaySolarRadio .
:Query1 dc:coverage onto:Audio .
:Query1 dc:coverage onto:Electronics .
```

Figure 8.4: Metadata with inferred triples

The "knack" used in our approach is to define the properties subcategory, etc., as subproperties of dc:coverage and to define dc:coverage as transitive. The property dc:creator is handled similarily. As a consequence, the inference engine enhances the metadata from figure 8.1 with extra implicit triples. For Resource1 this results in an implicit dc:coverage for the Audio subcategory and the Electronics category. Figure 8.4 shows the enhanced metadata for Resource1 and Query1 with inferred triples in italic.

8.3 Set-based Similarity Measure

In order to compute a search ranking we need a similarity measure that defines the distance between two (a query and a resource) descriptions. RDF descriptions consist of a set of property-value pairs. The obvious naive approach is to compare these sets and to define the similarity as the number of pairs that occur in both descriptions relative to the total number of distinct

Table 8.1: Match values for the sample queries

	Resource1	Resource2	Resource3	Resource4
Query1	1	0	.6	.4
Query2	0	0	0	1
Query3	.6	0	1	.286
Query4	.4	0	.286	1

pairs. For example, the similarity between `Query1` and `Resource1` from figure 8.4 would be $\frac{3}{7} = 0.4286$ as 3 property-value pairs exists in both and 7 property-value pairs exist in either description.

Formally, let R be the RDF repository containing a set of triples $t = (r, p, v)$, with the functions $subj(t)$, $pred(t)$, $obj(t)$ for the subject, predicate, or object of triple t. Also, let $D(r)$ be the RDF description of a resource r, i.e. $D(r) = \{t \in R \mid subj(t) = r\}$. Finally, $D'(r)$ is defined as the set of property-value pairs from $D(r)$, i.e. $D'(r) = \{(p, v) \mid \exists (r, p, v) \in D(r)\}$.

$$similarity(r_{doc}, r_{query}) = \frac{|D'(r_{doc}) \cap D'(r_{query})|}{|D'(r_{doc}) \cup D'(r_{query})|}$$

This basic similarity measure has two shortcomings. First, properties with many (also inferred) values dominate properties with only few values. Second, as queries will usually contain only few properties, resources with a rich metadata set (i.e. with additional properties the user does not search for) will be penalized. Consequently, we have refined the measure to compute similarities for each property individually and to only consider properties that are included in the query. Those that only exist in the resource (e.g., `dc:title` in the example) are ignored. Note that for this reason – in contrast to usual similarity values used in fulltext retrieval models – the measure is not commutative. It is only suitable for query evaluation, not for computing similarities among documents, e.g., for clustering purposes.

Formally, in addition to the above, $P(r)$ is defined as the set of properties in $D(r)$, i.e. $P(r) = \{p | \exists (r, p, v) \in D(r)\}$. Also $D'_{p_j}(r)$ is defined as the set of property-value pairs from $D'(r)$ with property p_j, i.e. $D'_{p_j}(r) = \{(p, v) \in D'(r) \mid p = p_j\}$.

$$match(r_{doc}, r_{query}) = \sum_{p_j \in P(r_{query})} \frac{1}{|P(r_{query})|} \frac{\left| D'_{p_j}(r_{doc}) \cap D'_{p_j}(r_{query}) \right|}{\left| D'_{p_j}(r_{doc}) \cup D'_{p_j}(r_{query}) \right|}$$

The value for the above example (match between `Query1` and `Resource1`) is now $\frac{3}{3} = 1$ as `dc:title` and `dc:creator` are no longer considered. Table 8.1 shows all match values for the sample queries from figure 8.1. `Query1`, searching for resources dealing with the Freeplay Solar Radio product, finds `Resource1`, `Resource3`, and `Resource4` in that order. `Resource1` deals only with that particular product, while `Resource3` also deals with two other products. `Resource4` deals with (among others) the Audio product subcategory to which the Freeplay Solar Radio belongs. `Query3` is supposed to represent an implicit query run on the basis of the report represented by `Resource3`. This query finds the same resources but with a different ranking. `Resource3` is ranked higher as it is more similar to the query.

The definition of the *match* measure has been translated into an algorithm that assumes that the metadata is stored in a repository that supports an RDF query language to retrieve the result candidates. The algorithm has been implemented using the Sesame RDF repository[3] [BKvH02] and integrated into the INWISS knowledge portal prototype[4] (see chapter 11). The approach has been enhanced to allow wildcards in the query description (e.g., dc:title = "*sales*"). This requires a deviation from the underlying set theory, but gives a pragmatic support for CDFQ-FR fuzziness (Crisp Data, Fuzzy Query, Fuzzy Result) for properties with literal values (see section above). Details on the implementation and a first empirical evaluation are given in section 11.4.

8.4   Applying the Vector Space Model

The approach presented in the previous subsection is based on set theory, i.e. it compares sets of RDF property-value pairs at query time. The advantage of this approach is that a standard RDF repository can be used with no modification as no a priori indexing is required. And so far, we have achieved acceptable performance. However, we expect a possible performance degradation when dealing with larger data sets. Some improvements might be possible on an implementation level. However, for large-scale environments it should be more appropriate to directly apply the Vector Space Model (VSM) as described in section ??.

For properties with literal values this seems the natural approach and promises to provide better ranking as in this case we actually deal with classic fulltext. The overall idea for proper-ties with instance data is to use the possible values of a property (its domain) as vector dimen-sions. For each resource a vector per property has to be computed. The similarity is computed for each property individually and then combined like for the measure used in our set-based approach.

Recall the definitions from section 6.1. A document is represented by a vector $d_j = (w_{1,j}, w_{2,j}, ..., w_{t,j})$ with the weighted term frequency $w_{i,j}$ being defined as follows (again, with frequency $tf_{i,j}$, the number of documents N, and document frequency df_i for document j and term i):

$$w_{i,j} = tf_{i,j} \times log\left(\frac{N}{df_i}\right)$$

For our metadata-based approach we now need to compute an individual vector $d_{p_j,r}$ for each property p_j and resource r. For properties with literal values this can be achieved in the same way as for full-text documents, i.e. the t-dimensional space is defined by the vocabulary used for the property. For properties with resource values the dimensionality t is defined by the number of distinct values (i.e. URIs) used for the property. The term frequency can thus only be a binary 0 or 1 (depending on whether a triple with the corresponding value exists). A document frequency can be computed by counting the resources for which a triple with property p_j exists with the corresponding value.

In the above example, assume that for dc:coverage the possible values (i.e. ontology elements) only comprise the ones used in the example, namely { FreeplaySolarRadio, MicroFMRadio, ShowerCompanion, Audio, Comfort, Gadgets, Electronics, CC_Atlanta, Atlanta, SouthEast }, i.e. the dimensionality is 10 (in this simplified ex-ample, of course the full ontology contains much more elements). Using this "vocabulary" and a binary weighting (occurence/non-occurence of an element) the dc:coverage vectors for the resources from figure 8.1 (including inferred triples) are:

---

[3]http://www.openrdf.org
[4]http://www.inwiss.org

$$d_{\text{dc:coverage,Resource1}} = (\ 1\ \ 0\ \ 0\ \ 1\ \ 0\ \ 0\ \ 1\ \ 0\ \ 0\ \ 0\ )$$
$$d_{\text{dc:coverage,Resource2}} = (\ 0\ \ 0\ \ 0\ \ 0\ \ 0\ \ 0\ \ 0\ \ 1\ \ 1\ \ 1\ )$$
$$d_{\text{dc:coverage,Resource3}} = (\ 1\ \ 1\ \ 1\ \ 1\ \ 0\ \ 0\ \ 1\ \ 0\ \ 0\ \ 0\ )$$
$$d_{\text{dc:coverage,Resource4}} = (\ 0\ \ 0\ \ 0\ \ 1\ \ 1\ \ 1\ \ 1\ \ 0\ \ 0\ \ 0\ )$$

Now, assuming that the resources given in the example are the only ones in the system (i.e. $N = 4$), the vectors can also be based on the weighted term frequency as given above (i.e. considering the document frequency of a certain element, e.g., the document frequency of Freeplay-SolarRadio is 2 as Resource1 and Resource3 are annotated with it):

$$d_{\text{dc:coverage,Resource1}} = (\ .301\ \ 0\ \ 0\ \ .125\ \ 0\ \ 0\ \ .125\ \ 0\ \ 0\ \ 0\ )$$
$$d_{\text{dc:coverage,Resource2}} = (\ 0\ \ 0\ \ 0\ \ 0\ \ 0\ \ 0\ \ 0\ \ .602\ \ .602\ \ .602\ )$$
$$d_{\text{dc:coverage,Resource3}} = (\ .301\ \ .602\ \ .602\ \ .125\ \ 0\ \ 0\ \ .125\ \ 0\ \ 0\ \ 0\ )$$
$$d_{\text{dc:coverage,Resource4}} = (\ 0\ \ 0\ \ 0\ \ .125\ \ .602\ \ .602\ \ .125\ \ 0\ \ 0\ \ 0\ )$$

Likewise, the dc:coverage vector for Query1 is:

$$d_{\text{dc:coverage,Query1}} = (\ .301\ \ 0\ \ 0\ \ .125\ \ 0\ \ 0\ \ .125\ \ 0\ \ 0\ \ 0\ )$$

Note that, for example, the occurence of MicroFMRadio is considered to be more significant than the occurence of FreeplaySolarRadio, as only one resource is annotated with it.

In order to get a consolidated match value, we need to combine the cosine similarities of the individual property vectors:

$$match(r_{doc}, r_{query}) = \sum_{p_j \in P(r_{query})} \frac{1}{|P(r_{query})|} \frac{d_{p_j, r_{doc}} \cdot d_{p_j, r_{query}}}{|d_{p_j, r_{doc}}| \times |d_{p_j, r_{query}}|}$$

Based on the above vectors, the matches for the sample resources with regard to Query1 (which contains dc:coverage as the only property) are:

$$match(\text{Resource1}, \text{Query1}) = \frac{.122}{\sqrt{.122} \times \sqrt{.122}} = 1$$
$$match(\text{Resource2}, \text{Query1}) = \frac{0}{\sqrt{1.087} \times \sqrt{.122}} = 0$$
$$match(\text{Resource3}, \text{Query1}) = \frac{.122}{\sqrt{.847} \times \sqrt{.122}} = 0.380$$
$$match(\text{Resource4}, \text{Query1}) = \frac{.031}{\sqrt{.756} \times \sqrt{.122}} = 0.102$$

If you compare these results to the first row of table 8.1 (i.e. the results of the set-based approach), you will recognize that the values are slightly different, but – as expected – the ranking order is identical, i.e. the query still returns Resource1, Resource3, and Resource4 in that order.

As the vectors can be precomputed this approach should improve the search performance creating, however, the necessity for an indexing process. In addition, the use of the VSM paves the way to combine a metadata-based search with fulltext searching for textual documents.

As future work, we are implementing a metadata-based search engine building upon the Jakarta Lucene information retrieval framework[5] as an alternative to the one based on the above set-based approach (see section 11.4). The metadata from the RDF repository is indexed and RDF-based query descriptions are translated into Lucene queries (after being run through the

---

[5]http://jakarta.apache.org/lucene/

inference engine). Lucene supports multiple so-called fields per document, which are used to represent the individual RDF properties. Properties with literal values are treated like regular fulltext (analyzed using tokenization, stopword elimination, etc.). For properties with URIs as values (like dc:subject and dc:coverage) a special analyzer is used that leaves the values untouched.

As expected, the search performance appears to be higher than with the set-based approach, although an in-depth evaluation still has to be carried out. However, the index needs to be recreated whenever new documents are added or the ontology changes.

8.5   Summary

In this chapter we have presented an information retrieval approach for ontology-based metadata which provides fuzzy queries by utilizing the similarity of query and resource representations as known from IR models like the Vector Space Model (VSM). The approach currently implemented within our INWISS knowledge portal prototype (see chapter 11) is based on set theory as described in section 8.3, i.e. it compares sets of RDF property-value pairs at query time. A first empirical evaluation is given in section 11.4.

This approach is perfectly suitable for the purpose of our prototype; however we expect a possible performance degradation when dealing with real world scenarios with larger data sets. Hence, as mentioned above, we are implementing an approach directly based on the VSM as described in section 8.4 as future work. This new version of our search engine is based on the Jakarta Lucene information retrieval framework and will also allow a combination of metadata-based and fulltext queries for textual documents.

Chapter 9

Integration of External Content and Applications

An important task of an enterprise portal is the integration of the heterogeneous information sources of an enterprise (see chapter 3). Many of them are not part of the portal software itself but represented by external applications to which the portal provides a homogeneous user interface. There are different approaches how external content and applications can be integrated into portals. In this chapter we discuss the integration of web-based applications, the integration of static content by means of content syndication, the use of third party portlets, and custom portlet development as state-of-practice building blocks within the *suggestion phase* of our design effort. The need for a generic, semantics-aware inter-portlet communication mechanism will be identified as an open issue; a solution based on Semantic Web technologies (the main contribution of this work) will be presented in the next chapter.

In today's enterprises portal systems are increasingly deployed as a kind of "standard workplace" for empoyees. The intention of enterprise portals is an acceleration of communication processes as well as an improvement of the information supply. Employees exchange and share information and collaborate with partners and customers. Enterprise portals provide personalization, content management and search, as well as the integration of external content and applications (see chapter 3). Since the IT landscape in enterprises is usually shaped by many heterogeneous application systems, this task represents a large challenge and requires the employment of different integration techniques.

In the following we present approaches for the integration of web applications and content (content syndication) as well as techniques which apart from content also allow the integration of application functionality into the portal. This can be achieved by means of third-party or custom-developed portlets. As the portal market is so far characterized by a variety of vendors, whose solutions are usually not compatible with each other, standardization efforts have come up. The demand for standards comes both from enterprises, which deploy portals, and from vendors, who want to make their content and applications available for portal integration. Therefore we will put special focus on existing and emerging standards (in particular, RSS in section 9.2, the Java Portlet Specification and WSRP in section 9.3).

9.1   Integration of Web Applications

If applications with existing web interfaces are to be integrated into an enterprise portal, there are some rather straight forward techniques available. However, with those techniques the possibilities for modifying the visual appearance of the applications are limited. In addition, advanced techniques for user-level integration (through inter-portlet communication) are not available.

9.1.1   IFRAMEs

The simplest integration approach is the IFRAME technology, which is based on the inline frame concept of the HTML language [W3C99]. With a generic IFRAME portlet existing websites can be embedded into the portal with rather little effort. However, the webpages are inserted as they are and cannot be modified. The IFRAME is supplied to the client browser together with a source URL. The browser establishes a separate connection to the source application and inserts the application markup into the IFRAME window. Hence, the aggregation of the webpage takes place within the client browser rather than the portal server software [WL03].

IFRAMEs represent a simple method for integrating external content into a portlet, however, this approach should be regarded critically. IFRAMEs present content based on a URL which must be accessible to the client browser. The portal server cannot guarantee whether the browser is allowed and able to establish a connection to the source since firewalls may intercept the communication. In addition there is no possibility for the portlets to communicate with each other as they run in completely separate server environments.

The IFRAME technology is useful if the integrated applications are subject to frequent changes, since the integration effort is extremely small.

9.1.2   Web Clipping

Besides IFRAMEs, a technique called "web clipping" can be used to integrate an (external) website into the portal. In this case the integration takes place on the portal server, not within the browser.

A simple form of web clipping which allows integrating complete websites (without tackling their visual appearance) is often available through a so-called webpage portlet. The server requests the content from the source application via HTTP and merges it into the portal page. For this purpose certain HTML elements (mainly the <html> and <body> tags) are removed. Additional modifications may be necessary. In particular, links within the webpages need to be rewritten such that they point to a URL that is interpreted by the portal server rather than the source application. As in this case the portal server acts as a kind of intelligent proxy, only the connectivity from the portal server (rather than the individual client browsers) to the application needs to be assured. In addition, content caching becomes possible [TKL+03, p. 256].

More powerful web clipping approaches offer more modification features than just removing certain HTML tags. Certain content areas can be selected using a special tool and are then made available within a portlet. Unwanted or redundant information (e.g. navigation elements) can be eliminated. Sometimes also certain modifications in the appearance of the selected fragment are possible to match it to the desired portal look-and-feel. With link rewriting (see above) it is possible to navigate to follow-up pages of the integrated application. Web clipping can provide the possibility to clip such pages in a specific way as shown in figure 9.1 [DeW02].

Hence, this technology provides a a fast and simple approach for embedding functionality and content of almost any web application into a portal. However, a restriction of the web

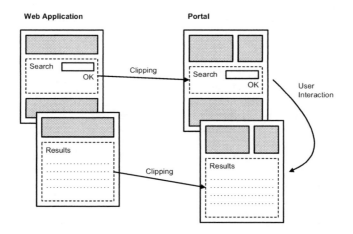

Figure 9.1: Web clipping with user interaction

clipping approach is that no permanent cookies can be used as it is the portal server rather than the client browser that communicates with the application. In addition, the application behind the integrated fragment is still treated as a "black box", i.e. the same limitations for portlet communication and integration apply as for IFRAMEs (see above) [DeW02, WL03].

9.2 Content Syndication

A further integration technique, which is however only suitable for integrating static information and messages, is content syndication. Content syndication allows exchanging content between different websites on the basis of news or information feeds.

Apart from portals such feeds are also used by desktop readers. Here the user has the possibility to present messages from different providers aggregated locally on his computer. The original motivation was however the use for portals, which present headlines and links from other websites, in order to provide an overview of different information sources. Netscape was the first to use this technology for its My Netscape portal[1]. Netscape tried to convince other website owners to provide their headlines as feeds so they could be merged into the portal. As an information format for these headlines Netscape defined RSS [Ham03, TKL+03, p. 264].

Meanwhile RSS can be seen as a de-facto standard for content syndication on the Internet. The acronym RSS stands for "RDF Site Summary", "Really Simple Syndication", or "Rich Site Summary", depending on the version. The different versions result from the developing history of the format.

The first official version of RSS was 0.90, developed by Netscape to integrate news headlines into their portal. RSS 0.90 is a simple application of RDF [W3C04d] which is why it was called "RDF Site Summary". RSS 0.90 was however only used for a short period of time; it was succeeded by RSS 0.91 which is the most well-known version. As RSS 0.91 is no longer conform with RDF for simplicity reasons, it was hence called "Really Simple Syndication".

---

[1]http://my.netscape.com

The company Userland[2] took over after Netscape had given up the development and released RSS 0.92 with slight modifications [Ham03, p. 26].

The RSS version 1.0 was developed independently of Netscape and Userland by the RSS-DEV Working Group[3]. This version, which is again based on RDF (and again called "RDF Site Summary"), supports namespaces and the inclusion of optional modules. RSS 1.0 is, however, not compatible with the predecessor versions 0.91 and 0.92 [Ham03, p. 55].

Finally, RSS 2.0 was developed as a direct successor of the older RSS 0.9x specifications. It stands under license of the Berkman Center at the Harvard Law School[4] and is called "Rich Site Summary". Like the 0.9x versions RSS 2.0 is not based on RDF [Ham03, pp. 3ff].

Despite the many versions RSS has evolved as a standard format for supplying information feeds on the Internet. Many online newspapers and magazines provide their headlines in RSS, weblogs are published in RSS, and more and more RSS-capable portal and client reader products have become available. Currently, the two standards 1.0 and 2.0 coexist side-by-side. Many tools can handle both of them (and sometimes even the 0.9x versions). In addition, a new format called ATOM, which tries to combine the advantages of the different versions, has appeared. Unlike RSS, ATOM is defined as an official IETF standard[5] and hence has good chances of becoming accepted. Besides RSS and ATOM, a number of other formats for content syndication were proposed, e.g. OCS (Open Content Syndication), PRISM (Publishing Requirement for Industry Standard Markup), and NITF (News Industry Text Format). They play, however, no significant role in practice [Gur03, p. 85].

Technically RSS is a simple XML-based format for exchanging messages and other content between websites. It allows websites and portals to include content from providers that make their content available as RSS feeds. An RSS document (also feed or channel), usually does not contain full content, but only metadata, text excerpts, and links to their HTML counterpart. A *channel* contains a number of individual *items* with a *link*, a *title*, and a *description*. An example (using the RDF-based RSS 1.0 encoding) is given in figure 9.2.

The rendering of RSS feeds on a portal server is handled by an RSS portlet. Usually a number of parameters can be defined, e.g. the maximum number of message entries or filters based on topics of interest. XSLT stylesheets are used to generate an HTML representation [TKL+03, pp. 264ff]. Using RSS feeds, external content can be integrated into a portal without any programming effort. RSS is capable of integrating static content, in particular news headlines; it is, however, unsuitable for integrating applications that require user interaction.

9.3   Third Party Portlets and Custom Portlet Development

The techniques presented in the previous subsections provide simple means for integrating external content and applications into portals. The integration is however limited to aggregating content on the portal user interface. Interactions between different sources are rather impossible. The reason is that the applications were originally not developed as portlets but as "normal" web applications. In order to utilize inter-portlet communication features, specific portlet implementations of the application user interfaces are needed.

With emerging standards like the Java Portlet Specification (JSR 168) and Web Services for Remote Portlets (WSRP) it can be expected that more and more software vendors will provide portlet implementations for their application products. If such third party portlets are

---

[2]http://www.backland.userland.com/rss/
[3]http://web.resource.org/rss/1.0/spec/
[4]http://blogs.law.harvard.edu/tech/rss/
[5]http://www.ietf.org/html.charters/atompub-charter.html

```xml
<?xml version="1.0"?>
<rdf:RDF xmlns:rdf="http://www.w3.org/1999/02/22-rdf-syntax-ns#"
  xmlns="http://purl.org/rss/1.0/">

<channel rdf:about="http://www.inwiss.org/news.rss">
  <title>News Feed</title>
  <link>http://www.inwiss.org/news.rss</link>
  <description>...</desciption>
  <items>
    <rdf:Seq>
      <rdf:li resource="http://www.inwiss.org/content/News_19980120.html"/>
      ...
    </rdf:Seq>
  </items>
</channel>

<item rdf:about="http://www.inwiss.org/content/News_19980120.html">
  <title>Electronics Bestseller Freeplay Solar Radio</title>
  <link>http://www.inwiss.org/content/News_19980120.html</link>
  <description>The Freeplay Solar Radio(TM) was our bestselling electronics
    product in 1997.  The crank-up radio never needs batteries -- it runs
    for an hour on a single crank up.  Solar power provides additional play
    time.</description>
</item>

...

</rss>
```

Figure 9.2: Sample RSS feed

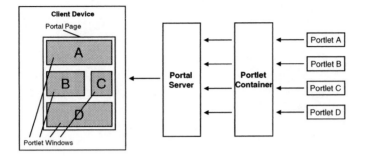

Figure 9.3: JSR 168-based portal architecture [JCP04]

not available it might be required to custom-develop portlets for certain applications. Also in this case, in order to stay vendor-independent, the mentioned standards should be applied where possible.

9.3.1   Java Portlet Specification (JSR 168)

The Java Portlet Specification [JCP04] defines an API for the development of portlets in a J2EE environment. This standard was established in order to simplify the integration of applications and back-end systems into enterprise portals. The increasing number of enterprise portals stepping into the market led to the development of many different portlet APIs, making it rather impossible for software vendors to provide universal portlet implementations of their applications as different versions for different portal platforms were required. This was the motivation for the Java Specification Request (JSR) 168, in which the Java Community Process (JCP) defines a standard API that guarantees the compatibility between J2EE-based portal platforms and third party application portlets [Hep03].

JSR 168 allows the interoperation of different portal platforms and makes it possible for developers to develop their portlets only once, universally executable on all JSR-168-compatible portal servers [MS04]. Actually, the specification distinguishes between a portlet container and the portal server itself. A portlet container runs portlets and provides them with the required runtime environment. It contains portlets and manages their lifecycle. However, it is not responsible for aggregating the content produced by the portlets. This is the responsibility of the portal server, which is however, out of the scope of the specification. This architecture is depicted in figure 9.3.

As already sketched in section 3.3, portlets can be seen as "pluggable" (in this case Java-based) software components, which produce either static or dynamic content fragments for the presentation within a portal user interface. The portlets communicate with the portal container via a portlet API, which can be seen as a contract between portlet and portlet container. Such a contract is the core of the Java Portlet Specification [JCP04].

The portlet container controls and manages the individual portlets. Portlets are addressed by request methods. The Java Portlet Specification differentiates two kinds of requests, an action request and a render request. An action refers to what is also known as action events in the Model View Controller (MVC) paradigm [BMR+96], i.e. events triggered by user interactions. An action can force a portlet to change its internal state. It must be terminated, before the rendering of the portlets on the portal webpage can be started. A render request forces the portlet to produce its markup fragment on the basis of its current state. The rendering of the portlets can take place in parallel [Hep03].

The Java Portlet Specification is based on the Java 2 Platform, Enterprise Edition (J2EE). Portlets have many similarities to Java servlets [JCP03], however, the JSR 168 expert group decided to define portlets separate from the servlet specification, mainly because the notion of actions should be inherent in the API and the portlet lifecycle. As we will see in chapter 11, this is very important. Mixing portlet action handling and rendering poses many problems, especially when dealing with inter-portlet communication, which is also a major drawback of the current Apache Jetspeed portal that we use for our prototype implementation (see chapter 11).

Portlets are Java classes that implement the `javax.portlet.Portlet` interface. The interface defines a `processAction()` method for action processing and a `render()` method that is called to retrieve the HTML fragment of the portlet. Altogether, the life cycle of a portlet consists of four phases:

- *Init:* At the time of portlet creation (i.e. when the portlet application is started, or delayed, when a user first accesses a portlet) a portlet's `init()` method is called.

- *Process action:* In response to an action request (usually triggered through a certain query string in the portal page URL), the `processAction()` method of the portlet is called, taking `ActionRequest` and `ActionResponse` objects as parameters. It is assumed that the portlet updates its state based on the information sent in the action request parameters.

- *Render:* During a render request, portlets generate content based on their current state. The portal container calls a portlet's `render()` method for this purpose. Here `RenderRequest` and `RenderResponse` objects are used as parameters.

- *Destroy:* When a portlet is taken out of service, e.g. when the user logs out from the portal application, the portlet's `destroy()` method is called. The portlet container is not required to keep a portlet loaded for any particular period of time. It might take it out of service, and recreate it at its convenience.

Even though the specification does not dictate how a portal performs the portal page rendering itself, it does strictly specify the above life cycle and the fact that the rendering is not supposed to start before all actions are processed (see figure 9.4). One important reason is that the specification allows portlets to change their window state (e.g. maximized) during action processing. In addition portlets may decide that the portal should send a redirect to a different URL back to the client. An HTTP redirect would no longer be possible if rendering had already begun.

The Java Portlet Specification is quite new, so it is not yet supported by all portal systems. However, all major vendors, including the Apache Software Foundation, have announced that future releases of their portal server products will conform to the specification (see section 3.4). As mentioned before, we use the Apache Jetspeed Portal for our prototype, which in its current versions does not conform to the specification. However, currently a new release Jetspeed 2 is under development, which builds upon of the portlet container Pluto[6], the reference implementation for the Java Portlet Specification.

The current version of the Java Portlet Specification does not define any particular means for inter-portlet communication. However, the separation of action processing and rendering is an important requirement to allow for portlet messaging. Portlets can invoke other portlets'

---

[6]`http://portals.apache.org/pluto/`

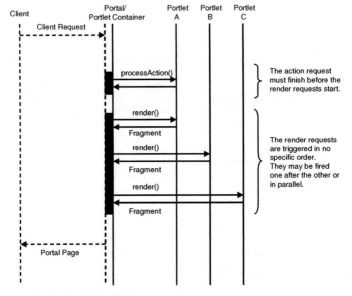

Figure 9.4: JSR 168 request handling [JCP04]

actions, possibly changing their state as well. If the rendering process would already have started, the target portlet of such a message might already be rendered, and the state change would not become visible before the next portal page reload.

More sophisticated inter-portlet communication capabilities are planned for future versions of the specification. As IBM is one of the main contributors in the JSR 168 expert group, the standard turns out to have many similarities to the API of the IBM WebSphere Portal [Hep03]. Hence, similar techniques like IBM's Cooperative Portlets and Click-to-Action technology (see as related work in section 10.1) might also appear in future versions of the Java Portlet Specification. Also, we will present our context-based integration approach as extensions to the Java Portlet Specification in the following chapter.

9.3.2 Web Services for Remote Portlets (WSRP)

Portals offer personalized access to information and applications. Typically portals receive the information from local or remote data sources, e.g. databases, transaction systems, content providers, or remote websites. Portals aggregate the information and present them on a consolidated webpage. This way the information can be delivered to the users in a compact and easily usable form. Apart from information, portals offer access to applications, such as email, host systems, ERP systems, content management systems, etc. [ST03].

Information resources and applications are represented by portlets, which we so far considered as software components that are locally installed on a portal server. This approach is practicable for realizing base services of a portal; however it is not well suited for a dynamic integration of business applications or external information sources. As an answer to this issue a new standard named Web Services for Remote Portlets (WSRP) was adopted by the OASIS standardization organization[7] [OAS03].

So far portlets were firmly installed on the portal server. WSRP tries to simplify the integration of remote content and applications into portals by making the portlets available as web services. Thus they can be integrated into the portal without being locally installed on the portal server. The characteristic of this approach is the distribution of functionality, i.e. the execution of the portlets takes no longer place on the portal server, but somewhere else on the network.

The envisioned application area of WSRP is the integration of information resources and applications from remote application and content providers on the Internet [ST03]. In order to achieve a simple integration, providers can offer their content as WSRP services and publish these services in a public UDDI directory. Portal operators that want to integrate certain information can look up a service, which supplies desired content, and integrate it. The integrated portlet is immediately available without programming and installation effort and can be used by the portal users. Besides the use by Internet content providers and portals the web service approach of WSRP obviously also makes a lot of sense for integrating applications into an enterprise portal within an organization.

WSRP utilizes the web service standards SOAP, WSDL and UDDI for communication, service description and discovery. This also provides interoperability between different programming languages and software platforms, i.e. the portlet server can run on a J2EE platform while the portlet runs in a .NET environment and vice versa. The communication between WSRP producer and WSRP consumer takes place via the SOAP protocol. The WSRP producer, which can be understood as a container for portlets, implements the WSRP interfaces and offers one or more portlets. The WSRP consumers are intermediate systems, usually portals, which present the WSRP services (i.e. portlets) to the users [OAS03]. This architecture is depicted in figure

---

[7]http://www.oasis-open.org

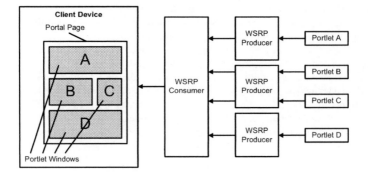

Figure 9.5: WSRP-based portal architecture

9.5.

WSDL is used in order to formally describe the WSRP service interface. WSRP can be regarded as a subclass of WSIA (Web Services for Interactive Applications), since both standards share fundamental common characteristics [ST03]. They both define a set of APIs, which permit applications to utilize remote interactive services. While the focus of WSIA is on a component model for the creation of interactive web applications, i.e. applications, which have their own web-based user interface, WSRP defines portal-specific interfaces.

The WSRP interfaces are very similar to the ones of the Java Portlet Specification. The standard defines a `Markup` interface with a `getMarkup()` operation, which the consumer uses to retrieve the HTML fragment of a portlet. A `performBlockingInteraction()` operation provides action handling, which is as such decoupled from the rendering process like in the Java Portlet Specification. WSRP portlets can be stateless or stateful. If they decide to be stateful, i.e. store some kind of session state locally, they send a session ID back to the consumer. The life cycle of a WSRP portlet session is as follows:

- *Init:* There is no explicit initialization of a portlet session. When a (stateful) portlet web service receives a `getMarkup()` request without an existing session ID it is required to create a new session.

- *Process action:* Before rendering the `performBlockingInteraction()` is called by the consumer to invoke portlet actions. As for the Java Portlet Specification, a portlet can request a window mode change or a redirection as a response to a `performBlockingInteraction()` request.

- *Render:* When the actions have been processed, the consumer calls `getMarkup()` to acquire the portlet content.

- *Destroy:* The consumer may inform the producer that it will no longer be using a set of sessions by invoking `releaseSessions()`, however this is not required.

Like the Java Portlet Specification WSRP is not yet supported by all portal servers, however, it is very likely to be introduced in future releases (again, see section 3.4). The WSRP reference implementation is WSRP4J[8] by Apache and might eventually also find its way into Jetspeed.

---

[8]http://ws.apache.org/wsrp4j/

Also for WSRP, the standard so far defines no particular inter-portlet communication means; these might be included in future versions. However, like for the Java Portlet Specification, as action processing and rendering is separated, portlets may invoke actions on other portlets when handling an action. The extensions we propose in the next chapter conform well to the standard and could be incorporated into WSRP as well.

9.4 Summary

In this chapter we have presented a variety of techniques that today's portal systems provide for integrating unstructured content and application systems that access structured data. In order to in order to provide a "true" integration and a contextualized information supply, inter-portlet communication mechanisms need to be utilized. This requires specific portlet implementations of the application user interfaces. With emerging standards like the Java Portlet Specification and Web Services for Remote Portlets (WSRP) it can be expected that more and more application software vendors will provide portlet implementations of their user interfaces.

The available techniques for inter-portlet communication (which will be covered in more detail in the related work section of the next chapter) are, however, rather unsuitable for portlets that are provided as third-party (standard software) components, as they do not consider the semantics of the information to be exchanged. This is where Semantic Web technologies can come into play. In the next chapter we present a novel generic, context-based portlet integration approach which uses Semantic Web technologies to represent and exchange the user context; it is the main contribution of this work.

.

Chapter 10

Context-based Portlet Integration

This chapter covers the core proposal (*suggestion*) of the design research effort presented in this work, and hence its main contribution. The goal of an enterprise-wide situational and integrated supply with structured and unstructured information can be achieved by using the context of application portlets as input for a search engine. Aiming for a rather generic foundation, this chapter builds upon inter-portlet communication techniques to develop a context-based portlet integration approach, which can be used as a building block together with the semantic search engine presented in chapter 8.

Portals have become the de-facto standard for web application delivery. They provide a large variety of techniques for integrating unstructured content and application systems that access structured data. With emerging standards like the Java Portlet Specification and Web Services for Remote Portlets (WSRP) (see chapter 9) it can be expected that more and more application software vendors will provide portlet implementations of their user interfaces. However, in order to provide "true" integration and a contextualized information supply, inter-portlet communication mechanisms are required. If such capabilities are offered at all in current portal systems, they require extensive individual programming and are not suitable for portlets that are supposed to be deployed as standard software components, as the semantics of the exchanged information are not considered.

In order to provide a generic portlet integration mechanism we present an approach based on communicating the user context (i.e. a semantic representation of what the user sees on the user interface) among portlets, utilizing Semantic Web technologies for the context representation and back-end integration [PP03].

10.1   Related Work

In the EU-funded research project GOAL[1] [KMM00], in which we also were involved, the integration of data warehouse (or more precisely OLAP) technology and geographical information systems (GIS) was covered. The basic idea of the approach that was developed in the project is that a geographical OLAP dimension can be mapped to GIS objects such that geographic maps can be used to navigate through OLAP data. The approach presented in this chapter was inspired by and can be seen as a generalization of this idea of user-interface-level integration.

---

[1]Geographic Information Online Analysis, INCO Copernicus project no. 977071

Our context-based portlet integration is based on inter-portlet communication techniques. Inter-portlet communication was already shortly covered in chapter 3. The following subsections will present the more sophisticated solutions that are available in the IBM WebSphere Portal Server and the SAP Enterprise Portal in some more detail.

10.1.1 IBM WebSphere Portal Server

As already discussed in section 9.3, if the action processing and rendering cycles are separated, it is possible to use action events for inter-portlet communication by having an action handler of one portlet invoke actions of others. IBM relies on this approach for portlet messaging [LR02].

As mentioned before, the API of the IBM WebSphere Portal Server (release 5.1) is very similar to the Java Portlet Specification, however provides some additional features for portlet messaging [Hep03]. IBM provides a concept called Cooperative Portlets which builds upon portlet messaging with action events and adds advanced capabilities for managing the communication paths [RC03]. They no longer have to be explicitly coded. A Property Broker receives data and distributes it to the targets. Hence, Cooperative Portlets allow dynamic binding for portlet communication. The communication targets do not need to be known when the portlets are developed, only the data (consisting of properties and values) that is transmitted and its semantics. The communication paths are defined by configuring the Property Broker. The message transmissions can be triggered by the user clicking special symbols, which is why the technology is also called Click-to-Action (C2A). When the user clicks a C2A symbol, a context menu is shown which allows him to select the desired target. C2A also supports broadcasts and multicasts using predefined target configurations, so-called Wires. The C2A symbols can be included in the JSP (Java Server Pages) code of portlets by using a special tag library. For the receiving portlet, a special configurable action event is invoked.

Cooperative Portlets and Click-to-Action provide an elegant messaging mechanism. However, the interpretation of the messages and the back-end integration is not addressed. We borrow IBM's idea of special JSP tags for selective context push scenarios (see section 10.2.2).

10.1.2 SAP Enterprise Portal

The SAP Enterprise Portal (release 6.0) provides a Enterprise Portal Client Framework (EPCF) for client-side communication between iViews (SAP's term for portlets) [SAP02]. It allows for low-level messaging based on JavaScript and (if desired) Java applets. This way iViews can send messages to each other on the client, hence not requiring additional HTTP request/response cycles. For this purpose SAP uses a client eventing mechanism and a so-called Data Bag. The eventing is based on a publish/subscribe multicast communication. The EPCF provides an elegant solution to synchronize iViews on the portal page. Although the communication is configurable (i.e. message paths do not need to be coded into the iView), the semantics of the messages need to be defined and interpreted by the iViews. There is no underlying semantic integration like our context-based one. However such an approach could be built on top of the EPCF messaging mechanism.

Second, the Unification technology together with Drag&Relate, provides a drag and drop functionality to enable a user-oriented integration [SAP02]. Drag&Relate does not really constitute an inter-portlet communication mechanism, but allows dragging objects from an iView onto the navigation iPanel invoking certain navigation actions. For example, you can drag a stock item number from the order information of a Siebel CRM iView onto a link that opens the corresponding mySAP PLM iView [FK02]. As Drag&Relate relies on Unification it only works for special Unifier iViews (i.e. not for custom-programmed Java iViews). Unifier iViews

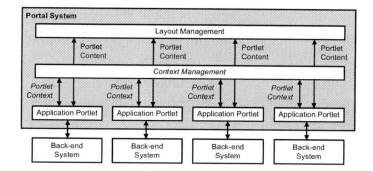

Figure 10.1: Architecture for context-based portlet integration

can be used to access (and combine) structured information from various data sources such as relational databases or legacy systems, provided a Unifier exists for this data source. The query processing is done by Microsoft's Distributed Query Processor (DQP) which is part of Microsoft SQL Server.

The core of the Unification (and Drag&Relate) technology is an integrated metadata model, the so-called Unified Object Model (UOM) and the so-called Correlation Matrix, which maps it to specific Application Object Models (AOM). This approach is similar to our ontology-based approach (see below). However, while we propose extensions to portlet APIs that allow custom-programmed portlets to participate in the integration, SAP provides this technology only for special (Unifier) iViews, without, on the other hand, requiring any extra programming effort. Note that Drag&Relate can only be used to integrate structured data from different sources, it provides no integration with unstructured data, i.e. the TREX search engine and content management module of the KM platform of the SAP Enterprise Portal (see chapter 7) are not accessible through Drag&Relate.

10.2 General Approach for Context Management

Recall the portal reference architecture form chapter 3. Usually portlets only provide their portlet content (usually an HTML fragment) for rendering the user interface. The layout management base service of the portal is responsible for consolidating this content to a portal webpage. We introduce an additional *context management* base service, where portlets can publish their current context, i.e. a semantic representation of the portlet content. Other portlets can retrieve that context and use it, for example, to display related information. Figure 10.1 shows the overall architecture of the proposed context-based portlet integration approach.

10.2.1 Capturing the Portlet Context

In chapter 2 context has been broadly defined as "any information that can be used to characterize the situation of an entity" [DA99], in this case a portal user. We have already identified the main challenges as defining a proper context model, automatically recognizing the user's current context, and deciding which elements are suited best to support him/her in a certain context [Kle00].

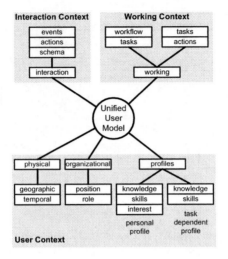

Figure 10.2: Unified user model for context information [HM03]

Henrich & Morgenroth [HM03] define the unified user model shown in figure 10.2, which considers user, working, and interaction context elements for context-based information retrieval (see chapter 2):

- The *user context* represents the physical context (location, time) of the user, his personal profile including his interests and skills in selected topics as well as the organizational position (leading, e.g., to specific user privileges).

- The *working context* characterizes the current tasks and actions a user needs to accomplish with regard to available material or immaterial tools (e.g., information systems and methods, the role of the user in a business process, information relevant for completion of a task).

- The user's *interaction context* reflects past and current interactions with the application system (e.g., selected menus or dialogs).

With regard to this user model we so far concentrate on interaction context elements. A user context can however be easily added as (more or less statically) modeled and bound to a user's identity or role. A working context is so far not considered as we cannot assume the existence of a structured representation of the user tasks. However, the integration of workflow technology for this purpose is subject to future research (see chapter 12). An approach for capturing the working context based on the concept of knowledge stances is presented in [HP05].

In our terminology, the interaction context is represented by a number of *portlet contexts* (i.e. the context bound to a portlet instance). We define the *portal context* as the combination of all active portlet contexts. We distinguish context pushes and context pulls. Context pushes are initiated by user interactions with a certain portlet and hence include the (full or partial) portlet context of this portlet. In a context pull a portlet can query individual portlet contexts or the overall portal context from the context management service. A detailed coverage of possible integration scenarios is given in the next subsection.

	Dollar Sales			
	Q1 1998	Q2 1998	Q3 1998	Q4 1998
Audio	$ 801.00	$ 457.00	$ 85.00	$ 372.00
Comfort	$ 10,461.00	$ 1,794.00	$ 3,385.00	$ 6,995.00
Gadgets	$ 2,508.00	$ 726.00	$ 756.00	$ 959.00

Reporting

Reports / Sales / Electronics Sales 1998

Figure 10.3: Sample reporting portlet

In order to be able to map the semantics of context elements between portlets, we base our approach on Semantic Web standards and technologies (see chapter 4). The main idea is to use RDF to represent the context, i.e. portlets should annotate their content with RDF metadata. For example, if a user displays an OLAP report [CD97] like the one in figure 10.3, the context can be represented as the set of elements (e.g., product categories) shown on the report like in the RDF code in figure 10.4, or a portlet representing a customer relationship management (CRM) system displaying information about a certain customer can point to a customer object to represent its context.

The anonymous RDF description of the context represents the elements shown on the report by identifying them with URIs. OWL concept mapping [W3C04a], e.g., `owl:equivalentClass` and `owl:sameAs`, and an inference engine can be used to map the concepts used by the context provider (in this case a business intelligence system) to business objects from an enterprise ontology. Hence, the portlets can use their own "language" to represent and interpret the context. This approach was already discussed with respect to metadata integration in chapter 7. For example, the product subcategory identified by the URI `http://www.microstrategy.com/elements/Subcategory_1` could be mapped to `http://www.inwiss.org/ontology#Audio`. In addition, the property `mstr:element` may be considered as semantically identical with `dc:coverage`.

As mentioned above, a major application for the proposed context-based portlet integration is to provide implicit "find related" searches based on the current context. A search initiated by the above portlet context from figure 10.3, for example, should also find the Freeplay Solar Radio brochure document, which we used as an example in chapters 5 and 8, as being related, because it is annotated as dealing with the Freeplay Solar Radio product (see figure 5.6 on page 62) which belongs to the Audio subcategory[2].

10.2.2 Context Integration Scenarios

Our proposal allows different context integration scenarios, distinguished by the four dimensions shown in the morphological box in figure 10.5:

- The first dimension is the *communication paradigm*. As already mentioned, context integration can follow a push or a pull principle. An example for a *context pull* is a search engine that queries the context of the other portlets to enhance the precision of the search results. *Context pushes* provide a semantic portlet messaging technique.

- For context pushes, the *triggering event* can be generic, explicit or implicit. For *generic* context pushes, we propose a generic "send to" control in the portlet title bar (see in figure

---

[2]With regard to the example in chapter 8, this refers to `Query4` that also finds `Resource1`.

```
<?xml version="1.0"?>
<rdf:RDF xmlns:rdf="http://www.w3.org/1999/02/22-rdf-syntax-ns#"
  xmlns:mstr="http://www.microstrategy.com/terms/">

<rdf:Description>
  <mstr:folder rdf:resource="http://www.microstrategy.com/folders/Sales"/>
  <mstr:metric rdf:resource=
    "http://www.microstrategy.com/metrics/DollarSales"/>
  <mstr:element rdf:resource=
    "http://www.microstrategy.com/elements/Quarter_199801"/>
  <mstr:element rdf:resource=
    "http://www.microstrategy.com/elements/Quarter_199802"/>
  <mstr:element rdf:resource=
    "http://www.microstrategy.com/elements/Quarter_199803"/>
  <mstr:element rdf:resource=
    "http://www.microstrategy.com/elements/Quarter_199804"/>
  <mstr:element rdf:resource=
    "http://www.microstrategy.com/elements/Subcategory_1"/>
  <mstr:element rdf:resource=
    "http://www.microstrategy.com/elements/Subcategory_7"/>
  <mstr:element rdf:resource=
    "http://www.microstrategy.com/elements/Subcategory_9"/>
</rdf:Description>

</rdf:RDF>
```

Figure 10.4: Sample portlet context

10.7 below) provided by the portal platform. *Implicit* context pushes are triggered implicitly by other (e.g., navigating) action events. For example, a taxonomy-based navigation portlet might publish the selected topic after every browsing event. Only for *explicit* cases the context transmission needs to be explicitly considered in the (action handling) portlet code. A context pull can only be explicit, as it also has to be included in the portlet implementation. We propose a "wire" concept which allows a declarative configuration of the source and target portlets in the next subsection, i.e. even for explicit scenarios the portlet developer will not have to know which other portlets are available in the portal.

- Context pushes can be transmitted as *unicast* (with a single portlet as the destination), as *multicast* (with a set of target portlets), or as *broadcast* (to all other portlets). For context pulls, it is not the target that varies, but rather the context source, i.e. the context of an individual portlet, a number of portlets, or all portlets can be queried. Again, we propose a context wire concept for configuring the communication paths in the next subsection.

- Finally, the portlet context that is considered can be *full* (covering all information that is shown within a certain portlet), or *selective* (covering only part of the portlet content). A selective context push can only be explicit, as it requires the user to select the part of the context that should be published. This needs to be arranged for by the portlet. An example for a selective context push is a "send to" button next to a customer name in a customer list that triggers a CRM portlet to display related customer information.

Note that not all combinations of all characteristics are possible, e.g., a context pull can only be full and explicit. Proposals for extensions to current portal standards and platforms that allow the realization of the mentioned scenarios are presented below in section 10.3. Examples

Communication Paradigm	Context Push		Context Pull
Triggering Event	Generic	Implicit	Explicit
Transmission Type	Unicast	Multicast	Broadcast
Considered Portlet Context	Full		Selective

Figure 10.5: Morphological box of context integration scenarios

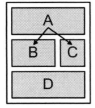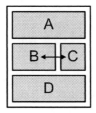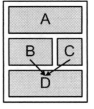

Figure 10.6: Sample context wires

for context integration scenarios that were implemented in the INWISS prototype[3] [Pri04] are given in chapter 11.

10.2.3 Context Wires

As already mentioned above, we propose a "wire" concept for configuring the context communication paths. The idea of wires is borrowed from IBM's Click-to-Action technique (see section 10.1). It allows grouping a number of source and target portlets and identifying this group by a name. Figure 10.6 shows three sample context wires: in context wire 1, portlet A sends its context to portlets B and C, context wire 2 defines a bidirectional coupling between portlets A and B, wire 3 has portlets C and D as sources and portlet B as the target.

Generic context pushes are initiated by the user clicking a special "send to" control in the portal title bar. It is expected that the portal provides the user with a menu which allows him to select from the wires available for this portlet as shown in figure 10.7. It shows the context wire menu for portlet B in the above example (which is defined as a source for wire 2 and 3). When using generic or implicit triggering, the portlet will not have to deal with selecting the context communication paths. In explicit scenarios (for implementation details see section 10.3 below) the portlet code will be able to identify the target of a push or the source of a pull by means of those wires.

In order to be potentially able to map context wire names (which might be encoded into portlet implementations as placeholders for possible envisioned integration scenarios) we also base the definition of the context wires on RDF. Figure 11.4 shows the definition of the above sample context wires from figure 10.6 in RDF/XML. In addition, it specifies, that context wire 1 is triggered by implicitly by "browse" action events, wires 2 and 3 are triggered in a generic fashion (see above). If no contextTrigger would be given for a certain wire, context

---

[3]http://www.inwiss.org

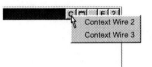

Figure 10.7: "Send to" control with context wire menu

pushes using this wire could only be triggered explicitly in the portlet code (for more examples, see chapter 11).

Context wires, portlets, and action events are represented as resources and identified by URIs. According to the Java Portlet Specification (JSR 168) and WSRP (see in section 9.3 and below), portlets are identified by a name. Some portal systems, e.g., the Jetspeed portal platform that is used for our prototype implementation (see chapter 11), use textual IDs and uniqely identify different instances of the same portlet (for different portal configurations). Obviously, the URI-based identification requires some adaption, in our prototype we simply extend the portlet instance ID with a leading namespace to get a portlet URI.

Action events are not explicitly mentioned in the portlet standards JSR 168 and WSRP; it is up to the portlet to distinquish and handle different types of actions. However, it is a common approach to use a textual action name as a parameter in the query string of the link that initiates the action. This approach is even mandatory for the action handling of portlets based on JSP (Java Server Pages) templates in Jetspeed (see chapter 11). We require named action events for implicit context triggering (see below). Again, we use URIs for identifying actions, i.e. if the portlets use simple names, they again have to be extended to full URIs by adding a namespace.

10.3   Proposed Extensions to Portal Platforms and APIs

In order to describe the approach independently of a specific portal server product, we base our proposal on extensions to the interfaces of the Java Portlet Specification (JSR 168) and discuss a possible adaption for Web Services for Remote Portlets (WSRP) (see section 9.3). We have already mentioned that in order to support our context-based portlet integration approach, portal platforms need to implement an additional context management base service that handles context push and pull scenarios.

By introducing implicit and generic triggering and context wires, we try to minimize the implication for the portlet development itself. The goal is that interoperable portlets can be imlemented without taking the existence of specific other portlets in the portal into account. It should be possible to provide them as standard software components and integrate them in various portal environments.

10.3.1   Context-aware Portlet Development

Recall the JSR 168 `Portlet` interface from section 9.3.1. We propose to extend it by a `getContext()` method that is, similarly to `render()`, called by the portal container. While `render()` provides the content of the portlet as an HTML fragment, `getContext()` is required to provide the portlet context (i.e. its current semantic state) as an anonymous RDF description encoded in RDF/XML. It would be possible to simply include the RDF annotation in the HTML code provided by `render()`, however, separating the two seems to be the

```
<?xml version="1.0"?>
<!DOCTYPE rdf:RDF [<!ENTITY portlet "http://www.inwiss.org/portlets/">
  <!ENTITY wire "http://www.inwiss.org/wires/">
  <!ENTITY action "http://www.inwiss.org/actions/">]>
<rdf:RDF xmlns:rdf="http://www.w3.org/1999/02/22-rdf-syntax-ns#"
  xmlns="http://www.inwiss.org/schema#"
  xml:base="http://www.inwiss.org/schema">

<ContextWire rdf:about="&wire;ContextWire1">
  <contextSource rdf:resource="&portlet;PortletA">
  <contextTarget rdf:resource="&portlet;PortletB">
  <contextTarget rdf:resource="&portlet;PortletC"/>
  <contextTrigger rdf:resource="&action;browse"/>
</ContextWire>

<ContextWire rdf:about="&wire;ContextWire2">
  <contextSource rdf:resource="&portlet;PortletA">
  <contextSource rdf:resource="&portlet;PortletB">
  <contextTarget rdf:resource="&portlet;PortletA">
  <contextTarget rdf:resource="&portlet;PortletB">
  <contextTrigger rdf:resource="#GenericContextTrigger"/>
</ContextWire>

<ContextWire rdf:about="&wire;ContextWire3">
  <contextSource rdf:resource="&portlet;PortletB">
  <contextSource rdf:resource="&portlet;PortletC">
  <contextTarget rdf:resource="&portlet;PortletD">
  <contextTrigger rdf:resource="#GenericContextTrigger"/>
</ContextWire>

</rdf:RDF>
```

Figure 10.8: Sample context wire definition in RDF

cleaner approach. The corresponding request and response objects of `getContext()` are assumed to be of type `ContextRequest` and `ContextResponse`, like `RenderRequest` and `RenderResponse` for `render()`.

Note that in the presented approach it is fully up to the portlet developer to decide how to represent the context as long as he/she uses RDF, or more precisely an anonymous RDF description with a set of properties and values (like for the above example in figure 10.4). It is desireble to use URIs also as values in order to be able to apply ontological mapping.

For handling (receiving) context push events, the regular `processAction()` could be used. However, as it is intended for user-triggered requests, we instead propose an additional `acceptContext()` method that the portlet can implement to accept context pushes. The request and response objects will be of type `AcceptContextRequest` and `AcceptContextResponse`. The request object will provide the URI of the context wire used for the context push (see section 10.2.3), the source portlet, and – most importantly – the pushed context in RDF/XML. The response object is identical to the one for regular action processing.

The same approach can be taken for WSRP, i.e. the `Markup` interface (see section 9.3.2) can be extended by `getContext()` and `acceptContext()` operations. These two methods are actually all the portlet developer has to deal with for generic and implicit (full) context pushes; the context wires (and potentially triggering events) are configured declaratively.

10.3.2 Explicit Context Pushes and Context Pulls

Generic context pushes are triggered by a "send to" control in the portlet title bar, implicit ones by action events that the portlet uses for other purposes. They can thus be initiated by the portal infrastructure, requiring no specific portlet code. Explicit context pushes, however, need to be triggered explicitly by the portlet in its action handler. The Java Portlet Specification (JSR 168) defines a `PortletContext` interface that portlet container provides to portlets giving them access to the portal runtime environment (which in our case includes the new context management service). This interface can be extended by a `pushContext()` routine, taking the target portlet or a context wire URI as a parameter. If a portlet URI is given, the corresponding portlet is the only target of the push, if a context wire URI is given, the specified targets of that wire are used. Note that as JSR 168 specifies the use of simple portlet names while we propose the use of URIs, a mapping (e.g., by adding a leading namespace) has to be performed.

When `pushContext()` is used within a portlet action handler for initiating a context push, the portal system will take care of executing the corresponding `acceptContext()` routine of the target portlet(s). Note that this is only possible, because the action handling and rendering cycles are properly separated in JSR-168-compliant portal systems (see section 9.3).

Selective context pushes can only be explicit. By definition they require the user (or at least the portlet) to select the part of the context that is supposed to be considered. Hence, the `pushContext()` routine can take a context description RDF/XML as a second (optional) parameter. If it is specified, the given context is pushed instead on the one provided by the portlet's `getContext()` routine.

Usually, some extension to the portlet user interface will be required to leverage the selection of the relevant context part, e.g., by adding a "send to" button next to certain content elements. If a template engine like Java Server Pages (JSP) is used, it is possibly to simplify this task for the portlet developer by providing a special JSP tag library. This approach is again similar to the one provided by IBM with Click-to-Action [RC03]. For example, an `<inwiss:contextPush>` tag could be used as shown in figure 10.9. The example shows the JSP code for a customer list from a CRM portlet, adding a "send to" button

```
<table>
  <tr>
    <th>Customer No</td>
    <th>Name</td>
    <th>Address</td>
    <th>City</td>
  </tr>

<%
  // some Java code to iterate through customer objects
  ...
%>

  <tr>
    <td><%=customer.getCustNo()%></td>
    <td><%=customer.getName()%>
      <inwiss:contextPush
        inwiss:wire="http://www.inwiss.org/wires/FindRelated">
        <customer xml:ns="http://www.siebel.com/terms/" rdf:resource=
          "http://www.siebel.com/customers/<%=customer.getCustNo()%>">
      </inwiss:contextPush>
    </td>
    <td><%=customer.getAddress()%></td>
    <td><%=customer.getCity()%></td>
  </tr>

...

<table>
```

Figure 10.9: Sample JSP code for selective context pushes

next to each customer name to push the customer object, say, to a search engine. Like for the product categories in the above example in figure 10.4 we assume that the customer URIs http://www.siebel.com/customers/<CustNo> (where <CustNo> represents an enterprise-wide unique customer number) are mapped to customer objects from the ontology by using the owl:sameAs property.

For context pulls, the PortletContext interface of the portlet container is expected to be extended by a getPortletContext() method that takes a portlet or context wire URI as a parameter. If a portlet URI is provided, the the portlet context of the given portlet will be retrieved. If a context wire URI is used as a paramter, getPortletContext() will retrieve the combined context of all source portlets of the given wire. Finally, if the parameter is omitted (or null) getPortletContext() will return the combined context of all active portlets in the current user session.

Explicit context pushes and context pulls are difficult to realize in a remote portlet (WSRP) environment, as there is no mechanism for the portlet web service to call the consumer. If a context pull is required, one way would be to include the complete portal context (i.e. of all active portlets) in every getMarkup() and performBlockingInteraction() request. Alternatively, the portal can offer a context management web service that provides the above getPortletContext() operation. In this case, the portlet (WSRP producer) can send a request to the context management web service of the portal (WSRP consumer) – hence reversing the request direction. The same approach would be necessary for explicit context pushes, i.e. the context management web service would need to provide a pushContext() operation.

10.4   Summary

We have presented an approach for utilizing a semantic user context for inter-portlet communication. The advantage of this approach is that portlets can be developed without taking into account with which other portlets they might be integrated. As opposed to other existing inter-portlet communication techniques, which only address the communication paths, we also present a way to handle the exchanged information, including its semantics, in a generic way. We use Semantic Web technologies to capture the context and propose a context management service that is capable of supporting different (push and pull) communication scenarios.

In order to be independent of a specific portal server product, the approach has been presented as proposed extensions to the Java Portlet Specification (JSR 168) and Web Services for Remote Portlets (WSRP). In addition, it has been implemented in the INWISS prototype using the Apache Jetspeed portal platform as a basis. Unfortunately the current version of Jetspeed does not conform to the Java Portlet Specification. Hence, there is a certain (however, not essential) gap between our proposal and its implementation. Details on the prototype follow in chapter 11.

So far we only consider the interaction context [HM03]. Future work will involve utilizing static user context elements and the integration workflow functionality (and/or support for knowledge stances [HP05]) in order to also regard the working context. Also, for the interaction (respectively portlet) context, we currently only consider the current state, i.e. we do not keep a context history. However, especially for context pull scenarios, also older context information might be of interest.

Part III

Evaluation and Future Directions

Chapter 11

Prototype "INWISS"

In order to evaluate the proposals from the previous chapters 5 through 10, we have implemented the INWISS knowledge portal prototype based on the Apache Jetspeed portal platform. This chapter discusses the implementation of the prototype and presents the results of the evaluation. Hence, it represents the *development* and *evaluation* phases of the design research effort covered by this work. The chapter closes with an evaluation summary and leads over to possible future directions which are then discussed in chapter 12.

Figure 11.1 shows the overall architecture of the INWISS portal prototype[1] [Pri04]; the individual components are described in the following sections. The implementation is based on the Apache Jetspeed portal platform[2]. Recall the portal reference architecture from chapter 3.

Apache Jetspeed (section 11.1) represents the layout management base service of the portal. Based on the Jetspeed portlet API the four portlets shown on the screenshot of the running prototype in figure 11.2 have been implemented (for details see section 11.2). One is responsible for displaying unstructured content (i.e. intranet articles). Our preliminary content management service (section 11.5) uses RDF metadata and a file-system-based content store. The navigation portlet represents a topic browser based on a taxonomy (structure management). A third portlet is responsible for metadata-based searches. The semantic search engine (section 11.4) retrieves candidate search results from the RDF repository and ranks them by their relevance to a user query. Finally, a fourth portlet views OLAP reports from a data warehouse [CD97]. We use this portlet as an example for an application portlet that accesses structured data through an external back-end system. Note that the reporting portlet has been implemented as if it was provided as a third-party software component, i.e. it does not consider the existence of any of the other portlets. The context-based portlet integration, which among others supports implicit searches generated from the current context of the reporting portlet, is provided by the additionally proposed context management service (section 11.3). The CSAP security module deals with authentication and access control issues [PMDP04]; it integrates with the Jetspeed security mechanism and represents the portal's security base service.

The reporting portlet uses the MicroStrategy 7i business intelligence package[3] as a back-end system. On the data source layer, the open source Sesame RDF framework[4] [BKvH02] is used

---

[1]http://www.inwiss.org
[2]http://portals.apache.org/jetspeed-1/
[3]http://www.microstrategy.com
[4]http://www.openrdf.org

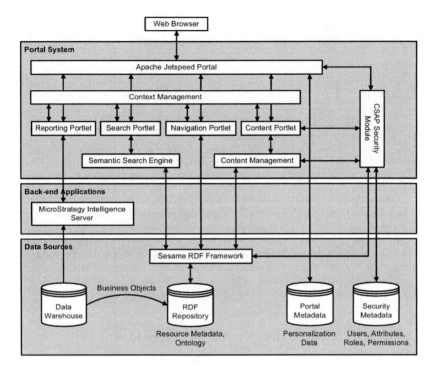

Figure 11.1: Prototype architecture

for managing the resource metadata, taxonomy, and ontology. An Oracle9i database[5] is used to store the data warehouse, the portal and security metadata, as well as the raw RDF data for Sesame.

11.1 Apache Jetspeed Portal

As already stated in chapter 3, Apache Jetspeed is a Java-based open source portal platform, providing support for XML/XSL and templating and content publication frameworks such as Java Server Pages (JSP), Apache Velocity[6], and Apache Cocoon[7]. The current release of Apache Jetspeed is 1.5, which is also the version used for our prototype. Currently, a new version Jetspeed 2 is under development, which offers several architectural enhancements and improvements over Jetspeed 1. Jetspeed 2 will be conformant to the Java Portlet Specification (JSR 168) and has a more scalable multi-threaded component architecture. We use Jetspeed 1, as so far no stable release of Jetspeed 2 is available. So, when we use the name Jetspeed we talk about Jetspeed 1.

---

[5]http://www.oracle.com/database/
[6]http://jakarta.apache.org/velocity/
[7]http://cocoon.apache.org

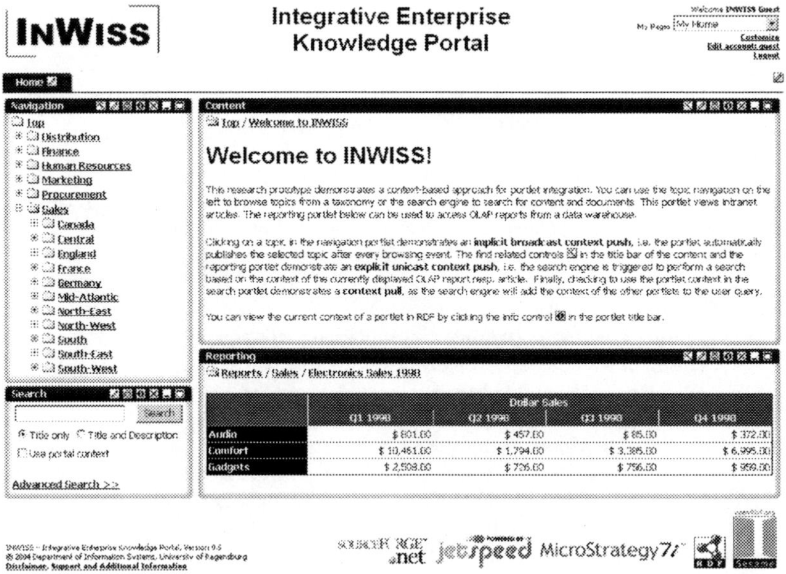

Figure 11.2: Screenshot of the running prototype

Jetspeed builds upon the Apache Turbine web application framework[8] and uses a servlet container such as Apache Tomcat[9]. User and personalization data is stored in a relational database and XML registry files. Jetspeed provides a runtime environment for portlets as well as a set of predefined portlets for syndicating HTML and XML data, as well as RSS feeds (see chapter 9). However, there is no expedient built-in content/document management or search functionality. For the INWISS prototype a custom content management service and search engine have been developed based on RDF metadata (see sections 11.4 and 11.5).

11.1.1   Portlet Development

Jetspeed portlets are Java classes that implement the Jetspeed `Portlet` interface which among others defines the method `getContent()` that is called by the portal to retrieve the HTML fragment for a portlet (like `render()` in JSR 168). A portlet can store its state in a Turbine `RunData` object. Jetspeed provides helper functions for getting and setting values in the `PortletSessionState` class. The life cycle of a portlet consists of three phases [Apa04]:

- *Init:* At the time of portlet creation, a portlet's `init()` method is called. It is only called once, during the portlet creation phase. The lifetime of a portlet is controlled by how long a portlet stays in the cache. When a portlet is removed from the cache, the portlet is effectively removed from memory and is no longer accessible. If a portlet is then requested again, the portlet will have its `init()` method called again, since a new instance of the portlet is created.

---

[8]http://jakarta.apache.org/turbine/
[9]http://jakarta.apache.org/tomcat/

- *Render:* The render phase is called per request. Every time a portlet's content is requested, the getContent() method is called.

- *Destroy:* The portlet object is destroyed when a portlet is removed from the cache. However, unfortunately the portlet is not notified when this occurs.

When the portal page is requested by the user's browser, Jetspeed iterates through all visible portlets from the top left-most down to the bottom right-most one, calls their getContent() method and sends the consolidated results back (see also below in figure 11.3).

Like already discussed in chapter 9, the usual way of developing portlets is to use the MVC (model-view-controller) paradigm [BMR+96], separating the handling of action events from the rendering. This paradigm is also used by Jetspeed, however, it unfortunately does not manifest itself directly in the Jetspeed portlet interface. Instead, actions must be handled in separate action classes together with a template engine like JSP or Velocity. This also leads to restrictions for inter-portlet communication (see below).

For a JSP portlet one has to define a JSP template (as the MVC view) and an action class (as the MVC controller) that handles action events triggered by the user. The action class has to be derived from JspPortletAction which defines an abstract buildNormalContext() method that has to be implemented by the concrete action class to set the portlet session state to be used by the template. Both, the action class and the template can use further business classes whose instances can be stored in the portlet session state. These business classes are then considered as the MVC model. Action events are triggered by a user event (i.e. a link or a form submit with certain parameters in the query string). For every portal page reload the framework checks the query string for the parameters js_peid (identifying the target portlet) and eventSubmit_do<Event> (where <Event> is the name of a user event), and calls the corresponding do<Event>() method of the corresponding action class. Consequently, the life cycle of a JSP portlet consists of the following four phases [Apa04]:

- *Init:* There is no explicit initialization for JSP portlets. The action class has to check the current portlet session state within the event handlers or buildNormalContext() for the necessity of an initialization.

- *Process action:* The corresponding do<Event>() method of the JSP portlet action class is called.

- *Render:* First buildNormalContext() of the portlet action class is called, then the JSP template is rendered.

- *Destroy:* Like for regular portlets, no notification occurs when the portlet is destroyed.

Note that, as the MVC paradigm is not inherent in the Jetspeed portlet API, but is only used by certain MVC portlets, the action processing and rendering phases always co-occur portlet by portlet. On a portal level, there is no separate action handling phase before the rendering starts. In other words, when the action event of a certain portlet is handled, other portlets have already been rendered. The process of rendering the portal page (with in this case four portlets) is depicted in figure 11.3.

11.1.2   Inter-Portlet Communication

Jetspeed does not provide any explicit techniques for inter-portlet communication. However, the portlets share a single Turbine RunData object. Usually, every portlet only accesses its

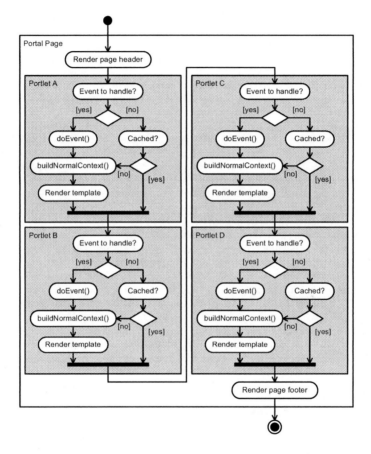

Figure 11.3: Portal page rendering process in Jetspeed

own session state through the mentioned PortletSessionState class. However, it is also possible to read and modify the state of other portlets. The second technical means that can be used to have portlets talk to each other is the action events. Theoretically, it would be possible to communicate something to another portlet by writing information into its session state in the RunData object and then call an event handler in the target portlet's action class to trigger an action event. This is what would be done with a portlet container that conforms to the Java Portlet Specification.

Unfortunately the missing separate event handling phase in Jetspeed defeats this approach. As stated above, portlets are rendered directly after their action events have been processed. If a portlet action handler decides to communicate with (and as a consequence change the state of) another portlet which has already been rendered, the state change will not be considered before the next rendering cycle. A second problem is posed by the caching mechanism of Jetspeed. Portlets are usually only rerendered, if the query string contains an action event to be handled by them, thus direct calls to another portlet's action class will not invalidate the cache. Action events thus need to be invoked by page reloads.

Usually, a portlet will only trigger its own events by building a query string with a js_peid parameter pointing to its own portlet ID. However, if a portlet knows the ID of another target portlet it can also trigger events of another portlet. By omitting the js_peid parameter, a broadcast can be realized, as all portlets will handle the triggered event. Encoding the inter-portlet communication in query strings within the template is, however, not desirable. A portlet template should usually trigger its own events and the action handler should then decide whether it wants to trigger another event for a target portlet. The only way to achieve this is by means of a redirect, that restarts the rendering cycle.

Both, the Java Portlet Specification (JSR 168) and Web Services for Remote Portlets (WSRP) standards include the possibility of redirects as a response to handling an action. Theoretically, this would also be possible in Jetspeed with the setRedirectURI() method of the RunData object. However, as Jetspeed has already started sending HTML back to the browser when the actions are handled, a regular HTTP redirect can no longer be sent to the browser. To overcome this issue the JspPortletAction behavior was modified in our prototype to send JavaScript redirects if requested by a portlet action handler.

With the help of the common RunData object and by triggering each others (or broadcast) action events, also from action handlers through redirects, various inter-portlet communication scenarios become possible. These were used in the prototype to implement some of the context integration scenarios discussed in chapter 10 (see section 11.3).

11.2   Demonstration Portlets

As stated above, four portlets have been implemented for demonstrating the proposals. Three of them represent user interfaces to portal base services (search, navigation/structure management, and content management). One (the reporting portlet) is an example for a portlet that accesses an external back-end application; it could have been provided as a third party software component. The four portlets are shown on the screenshot in figure 11.2.

11.2.1   Search Portlet

The search portlet provides a user interface to the semantic search engine (see section 11.4). It offers a simple and an advanced mode: In simple mode (as in figure 11.2), a user can search for the title and description only; the advanced mode allows searching for arbitrary metadata fields, requiring however more space on the portal user interface, switching the portlet to a maximized window state. The portlet communicates with the search engine via a simple, well-defined Java interface, which makes it easier to exchange the engine implementation, e.g., with the new VSM-based (Vector Space Model) version that is developed as future work (see chapter 8).

The search portlet accepts context events, using the received context as a search query. This provides for "find related" queries based on the context of an existing intranet article (content portlet) or OLAP report (reporting portlet). The context management implementation is covered below in section 11.3.

11.2.2 Navigation Portlet

The navigation portlet allows the user to navigate through a hierarchical taxonomy of topics. These topics can be seen as (virtual) folders according to which the resources of the enterprise are organized. The taxonomy is encoded in RDF and stored in the Sesame RDF repository. The portlet uses the Sesame API to access the repository via HTTP.

By means of a context push the navigation portlet communicates the currently selected topic to the other (in our case the content and reporting) portlets, which can then list the corresponding resources (intranet articles and OLAP reports).

11.2.3 Content Portlet

The content portlet is responsible for viewing intranet articles and for browsing the topics of the taxonomy. In the architecture diagram in figure 11.1 it communicates with a content management service. However, in our current implementation a real "service" for content management has so far not been implemented; the content portlet currently communicates directly with the metadata repository and a content directory on the file system. The resource metadata and the list of resources that are assigned to a certain taxonomy topic are retrieved via the Sesame API and HTTP from the Sesame RDF repository. The content itself is retrieved directly via file system access.

The content portlet accepts context pushes, e.g., from the navigation portlet, that point to a certain taxonomy topic. This topic is then opened in browsing mode, i.e. the intranet articles that are associated with this topic are listed. As a context provider, the portlet publishes the currently opened topic in browsing mode and the semantic metadata of the currently viewed article in viewing mode (see section 11.3).

Currently, the portlet offers no authoring or check-in/check-out functionality (see chapter 5), a fully functional content management component is however planned for future development (see section 11.5).

11.2.4 Reporting Portlet

The most sophisticated portlet is the reporting portlet which provides access to a MicroStrategy 7i server. It uses the MicroStrategy Java API to execute a report on the server. This is achieved via an HTTP-based protocol; the report results are received from the server encoded in XML. The portlet transforms the XML into HTML and presents the report to the user. In addition, the portlet provides browsing functionality for the folders on the MicroStrategy server, which are created in alignment with the taxonomy used by the navigation and content portlets. It is assumed that this is an enterprise-wide global taxonomy, different names can however still be mapped by means of ontological mapping (e.g., `owl:sameAs`).

Like the content portlet, the reporting portlet accepts context pushes that contain a pointer to a folder to be browsed. Likewise it provides a report context as the set of elements shown on the report (see section 11.3). Note that the reporting portlet contains no specific code that considers the existence of any of the other portlets whatsoever. Hence, it could have been provided as a third party software component.

11.3 Context Management Implementation

The context-based portlet integration approach presented in chapter 10 has been implemented as extensions to the Apache Jetspeed portal platform, providing basic means for context-aware portlet development and supporting generic, implicit, and explicit context push and pull scenarios, as well as context wires. Restrictions apply to generic context pushes as a menu selection of specific context wires (see section 10.2.3) is not realized. In addition there is so far no user interface (e.g., JSP tag library) support for selective context pushes (see section 10.3.2).

11.3.1 Extensions to Apache Jetspeed

Like we proposed in section 10.3 as an extension to the Java Portlet Specification and WSRP, we introduced a `getContext()` method to a modification of the `JspPortletActionClass`, called `ContextPortletActionClass`. The method is called by the event handler after the usual `buildNormalContext()` and the retrieved context RDF description is put into a `context` variable of the portlet's session state. In other words, the `context` variables in the `RunData` object together represent the context repository.

For context push events we introduced an `acceptContext()` method to the `Context-PortletActionClass`. Portlets that wish to receive context push events need to implement this method. The context in RDF/XML is given as a parameter together with the source portlet and context wire used for the push. Internally the action event `acceptcontext` and the above mentioned means from section 11.1.2 are used for inter-portlet communication, however this is transparent for the portlet developer.

In order to trigger a generic context push, an extra "send to" control was added to the portlet title bar. The user can click this control to invoke a context push. All that remains to be done for the portlet developer is to implement the `getContext()` and `acceptContext()` methods. Context wires are used to configure the communication paths. In the current implementation a user menu selection as proposed in section 10.2.3 is so far not realized. Instead the context wire that is triggered when the user clicks the generic "send to" control is configured using a portlet initialization parameter.

The `ContextManagement` service class provides a function `pushContext()` for initiating explicit context pushes. It takes a portlet or context wire URI as a parameter. If a portlet URI[10] is provided, this portlet is used as the target of the push. If a context wire URI is given, all target portlets of that wire are targeted. Due to the lack of separation of action processing and rendering in Jetspeed, a redirect is used to realize the push (see above in section 11.1.2). In addition, for context pulls, the `ContextManagement` class provides a `getPortletContext()` function allowing portlets to query the context of others. If a portlet URI is given as an argument, the context only of this portlet is returned in RDF/XML.

---

[10]Jetspeed uses IDs for identifying the portlet instances, e.g., `P-fe2fd4c6b4-10000` for the reporting portlet. These IDs are converted to a URI by adding a namespace, i.e. the reporting portlet is represented by the URI `http://www.inwiss.org/portlets/P-fe2fd4c6b4-10000`.

```xml
<?xml version="1.0"?>
<!DOCTYPE rdf:RDF [<!ENTITY portlet "http://www.inwiss.org/portlets/">
  <!ENTITY wire "http://www.inwiss.org/wires/">
  <!ENTITY action "http://www.inwiss.org/actions/">]>
<rdf:RDF xmlns:rdf="http://www.w3.org/1999/02/22-rdf-syntax-ns#"
  xmlns="http://www.inwiss.org/schema#"
  xml:base="http://www.inwiss.org/schema">

<ContextWire rdf:about="&wire;TaxonomyNavigation">
  <contextSource rdf:resource="&portlet;P-fe309b1531-10000">
  <contextTarget rdf:resource="&portlet;P-fe2a16446a-10001">
  <contextTarget rdf:resource="&portlet;P-fe2fd4c6b4-10000"/>
  <contextTrigger rdf:resource="&action;browse"/>
</ContextWire>

<ContextWire rdf:about="&wire;FindRelated">
  <contextSource rdf:resource="&portlet;P-fe309b1531-10000">
  <contextSource rdf:resource="&portlet;P-fe2a16446a-10001">
  <contextSource rdf:resource="&portlet;P-fe2fd4c6b4-10000">
  <contextTarget rdf:resource="&portlet;P-fd687b96a8-10001">
  <contextTrigger rdf:resource="#GenericContextTrigger"/>  .
</ContextWire>

<inwiss:ContextWire rdf:about="&wire;OpenResource">
  <contextSource rdf:resource="&portlet;P-fd687b96a8-10001">
  <contextTarget rdf:resource="&portlet;P-fe2a16446a-10001">
  <contextTarget rdf:resource="&portlet;P-fe2fd4c6b4-10000">
</ContextWire>

</rdf:RDF>
```

Figure 11.4: Sample context wire definition in RDF

If a context wire URI is given, the combined context of all source portlets of this wire is returned. Finally, if the portlet/wire URI is null or omitted, the combined context of all portlets is returned.

11.3.2 Demonstration Scenarios

As mentioned above, the portal configuration consists of four portlets: a navigation portlet used to browse topics from a taxonomy, a search portlet to search for content and documents, a content portlet to view intranet articles, and finally a reporting portlet that can be used to access OLAP reports from a data warehouse.

The navigation portlet publishes the selected topic as a Dublin Core dc:subject. In browsing mode the content portlet also publishes the currently accessed taxonomy topic, in view mode (i.e. when displaying an article) it in addition publishes the ontology elements from the article metadata as Dublin Core dc:coverage. The same is true for the reporting portlet, however it publishes the currently open folder as mstr:folder and the elements shown on a report as mstr:element; the corresponding mapping is done through the ontology. Note that these elements are dynamically retrieved from the report content, i.e. this also works for ad-hoc reports created by drilling and slicing/dicing.

The content and reporting portlets accept dc:subject (or mstr:folder) elements when receiving context push events, reacting by browsing the corresponding topic or folder.

The search portlet accepts arbitrary context elements, using them as a search query. The context wire configuration (see above) is shown in figure 11.4[11]; three wires are defined supporting four context integration scenarios:

- As defined in the `TaxonomyNavigation` wire, the navigation portlet publishes its topic to the content and reporting portlets (i.e. using a multicast). The context event is triggered implicitly by "browse" action events. This scenario represents a *full implicit multicast context push* as shown in the morphological box in figure 11.5.

Communication Paradigm	Context Push		Context Pull
Triggering Event	Generic	Implicit	Explicit
Transmission Type	Unicast	Multicast	Broadcast
Considered Portlet Context	Full		Selective

Figure 11.5: Topic navigation scenario

- The `FindRelated` wire defines the communication between the search portlet and the other portlets. When the user clicks the "send to" control in the portlet title bar of navigation, content, or reporting portlet, the search portlet reacts with a "find related" query. This second scenario represents a *full generic unicast context push* as shown in figure 11.6. For example, when triggering a context push from of the OLAP report shown in the reporting portlet in figure 11.2, the search portlet will find related resources using the semantic search engine (see next section) and display the search results as shown in figure 11.9.

Communication Paradigm	Context Push		Context Pull
Triggering Event	Generic	Implicit	Explicit
Transmission Type	Unicast	Multicast	Broadcast
Considered Portlet Context	Full		Selective

Figure 11.6: "Find related" scenario in content and reporting portlet

- The same `FindRelated` wire is used for a (full explicit "broadcast") *context pull*. When the user selects to use the portal context in the search portlet, the search engine will add the context of the other portlets to the user query. This is depicted in figure 11.7.

---

[11]The portlet IDs used in the figure are `P-fe309b1531-10000` for the navigation portlet, `P-fe2a16446a-10001` for the content portlet, `P-fe2fd4c6b4-10000` for the reporting portlet, and `P-fd687b96a8-10001` for the search portlet.

Communication Paradigm	Context Push		Context Pull	
Triggering Event	Generic	Implicit	Explicit	
Transmission Type	Unicast	Multicast	Broadcast	
Considered Portlet Context	Full		Selective	

Figure 11.7: Search engine using a context pull

- The `OpenResource` wire is used by the search portlet when the user selects a resource from the search results to open the resource in the content or reporting portlet (if an article or report is selected). The URI of the selected resource is pushed to content and reporting portlet (using a `dc:identifier` statement). This scenario represents a *selective explicit multicast context push* as shown if figure 11.8.

Communication Paradigm	Context Push		Context Pull	
Triggering Event	Generic	Implicit	Explicit	
Transmission Type	Unicast	Multicast	Broadcast	
Considered Portlet Context	Full		Selective	

Figure 11.8: Open resource scenario

11.4 Semantic Search Engine

The semantic search engine provides global searching by using a repository integration approach (see chapter 7); intranet articles, external documents, and business intelligence reports are represented by metadata in a central RDF repository. In order to cope with the ontology-based metadata used by our content management service (as well as the ontology-based queries provided by the context integration) it uses a similarity-based information retrieval approach as proposed in chapter 8.

Again, when triggering a context push from of the OLAP report shown in the reporting portlet in figure 11.2, the search portlets reacts with querying the search engine for the results shown in figure 11.9. As you can see, it finds the report itself with an (obvious) match of 100%; however, as discussed in chapters 8 and 10, it among others also finds a brochure for the Freeplay Solar Radio product which belongs to one of the product categories shown in the report.

11.4.1 Ranking algorithm

The current implementation of the search engine is based on the set-based similarity measure from section 8.3. The definition of the *match* measure has been translated into an algorithm that assumes that the metadata is stored in a Sesame RDF repository that infers RDFS/OWL semantics and supports the SeRQL query language [BKvH02]. A sketch of the algorithm is provided in figure 11.10.

First, the query description is run through the inferencer to generate the implicit query triples. Then a SeRQL query is built to retrieve all triples of candidate resources from the

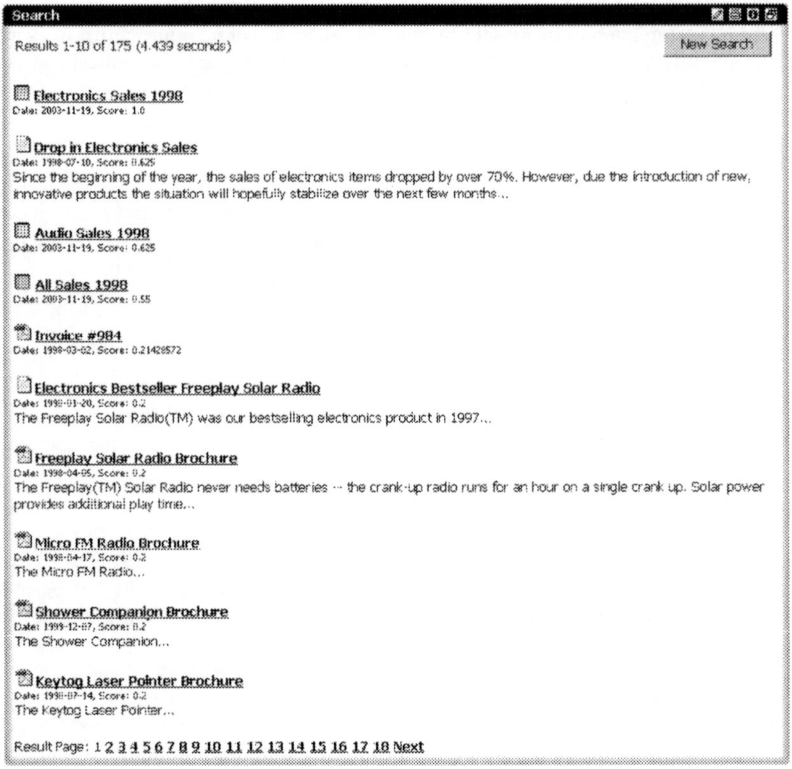

Figure 11.9: Search result presented by the search portlet

repository. For this purpose, the query property-value pairs are translated to WHERE clause constraints combined by a logical OR. Further computations are done in-memory on this set of candidate triples.

We iterate through all candidate resources and then through all properties from the query. For each property we compute a match and mismatch count which are then used to compute the match value for that property. The property match values are then combined to an overall match for the candidate resource. These match values can then be returned as ranking scores together with the candidate descriptions.

```
add query triples to repository and do inferencing
retrieve all query triples from repository
query properties := distinct properties from query triples
property count := number of query properties

start with query to retrieve all triples
for each query triple t do {
  add where clause for subject and object of t
}
retrieve query results as candidate triples
candidate resources := distinct resources from candidate triples

for each candidate resource r do {
  match value := 0

  for each query property p do {
    match count := 0
    mismatch count := 0
    remaining candidate property values := all values for resource r with
      property p

    for each query triple t with property p do {
      if corresponding triple exists for r {
        increment match count
        remove object of t from remaining candidate property values
      }
      else increment mismatch count
    }

    add number of remaining candidate property values to mismatch count
    add (match count / (property count * (match count + mismatch count)))
      to match value
  }

  memorize match value as score for r
}

return candidate resources with match values
```

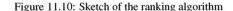

Figure 11.10: Sketch of the ranking algorithm

The algorithm has been enhanced to allow wildcards in the query description (e.g., dc:title = "*sales*"). This requires a slight deviation from the underlying set theory, but gives a pragmatic support for CDFQ-FR fuzziness (Crisp Data, Fuzzy Query, Fuzzy Result), which is highly desirable for properties with literal values (see chapter 8).

Table 11.1: Evaluation results

	Fuzzy Matches with Ontology	Exact Matches with Ontology	Fuzzy Matches w/o Ontology	Time Lag
Query1	221	1	221	2.199 sec
Query2	195	2	28	3.820 sec
Query3	175	80	1	3.547 sec
Query4	259	0	259	3.141 sec
Query5	458	5	219	6.543 sec
Query6	175	2	32	4.663 sec
Query7	175	4	4	2.222 sec
Query8	259	1	27	5.605 sec
Query9	175	1	4	3.977 sec
Query10	175	1	53	5.192 sec

11.4.2 Computational Complexity

The algorithm presented in the previous subsection consists of two parts. First, the query is added to the RDF repository and run through the inference engine and a SeRQL query to retrieve the candidate resources is built and evaluated by the RDF framework. Second, the retrieved candidates are ranked based on their similarity to the query description. The performance and complexity of the first part is rather a question of the RDF repository and its query engine than of our algorithm. As the empirical results in the next subsection show this, however, actually turns out to be the bottleneck of the approach. The second part, the ranking itself, is very fast and shows polynomial complexity.

Assuming that the set operations in the algorithm (finding all values for resource r with property p, checking whether a certain triple exists for resource r) have linear complexity with respect to the number of candidate resources, the whole ranking process shows quadratic complexity (i.e. the complexity is $O(n^2)$ where n is the number of candidate resources). Similarly, the ranking also shows quadratic complexity with regard to the number of search criteria specified (i.e. the complexity is $O(n^2)$ where n is the number of query property values).

11.4.3 Empirical Evaluation

In order to empirically evaluate the feasibility of our search approach, we have run the search engine against an RDF repository with 46.608 triples in total. The repository contains metadata for 1.322 (automaticaly generated) resources. The ontology consists of 23 classes (shown as a UML diagram in appendix A.1) and 2.421 object instances; the ontology was extracted from the data warehouse. 10 sample queries were used for the evaluation, given in N3 notation in appendix A.2. Query1 through Query5 are combinations of literal- and ontology-based user queries. Query6, Query7, and Query8 are "find related" queries based on existing documents, Query9 and Query10 based on OLAP reports, i.e. contexts provided by the reporting portlet. In fact, Query9 represents the query triggered by the above OLAP report shown in figure 11.2 with the results shown in figure 11.9.

In order to evaluate the quality of the results we compare them to exact queries which corresponds to what many document and knowledge management systems do for metadata searches. As discussed in chapter 8 we make use of inferred information that results from semantic links to an underlying ontology. In order to show the recall gain we get from doing so, we compare our results to those that can be achieved without using the ontology as well.

The right-most column of table 11.1 shows the time in seconds needed to retrieve and rank the results. We achieved acceptable performance on standard PC hardware, which is sufficient for our prototype. However, we expect a possible performance degradation when dealing with real world scenarios with larger data sets. Hence, we are implementing an approach based on the Vector Space Model as described in section 8.4 as an alternative to the set-based approach future work. The results in terms of recall and ranking are expected to be identical, but the approach achieves quicker search performance, however, with the cost of requiring a separate indexing process.

The left-most column of table 11.1 shows the number of matches found by our fuzzy algorithm. Our queries consist of a number of property-value pairs as search constraints. The number of matches corresponds to the number of results returned by a SeRQL query that uses these as a WHERE clause combined by a logical OR, which is actually what our algorithm does to find the candidates. However, keep in mind that without extra ranking such a query provides no ordering by relevance. The second column shows the number of matches for an exact query using a logical AND rather than OR. This leads to a rather strict query that returns only highly relevant results, however missing less (but still) relevant ones. Respectively, the fourth column of the table shows the match count that can be achieved by our fuzzy algorithm without using the ontology and inferred triples.

As we still work on generated test data, we so far cannot use any human relevance judgments. For the same reason we cannot give any actual recall and precision values. The result shows that the combination of inferred triples and a fuzzy search lead to a remarkable gain in recall. In addition, our ranking approach makes sure that all resources that fulfill all search constrains (those also found by a strict exact query) will receive a maximum match value. As a consequence they will be at the top of the ranked result list (avoiding a loss in precision). We are in contact with some companies, which will hopefully give us the chance to test our approach on real-life data in future.

11.5 Content Management Implementation

A real content management "service" has so far not been implemented; the content portlet currently communicates directly with the RDF repository and a content directory on the file system. The implementation of a more sophisticated content repository, most probably based on the Jakarta Slide project of the Apache Software Foundation[12], as well as authoring and check-in/check-out functionality is planned for future development. It will be combined with a semi-automatic approach for meta-data creation as proposed in chapter 6.

Figure 11.11 shows a screen design of a content management portlet with a metadata form that can be used for adding a new document to the system. When adding a new document the user would normally have to manually fill out all relevant metadata fields. With the help of a semi-automatic annotation approach the fields will be pre-filled where possible. The user then only has to check and if necessary correct the proposed values.

11.6 Evaluation Summary

The goal of this work was to analyze how Semantic Web technologies can help building integrative enterprise knowledge portals that provide integrated and situational access to structured

---

[12]http://jakarta.apache.org/slide/

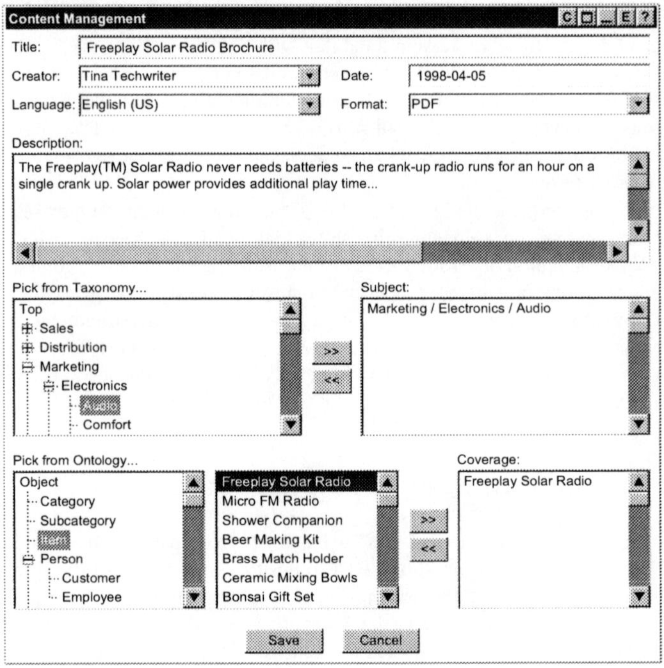

Figure 11.11: Content portlet with metadata for a new document

and unstructured information within enterprises. In this context we have made different proposals in chapters 5 through 10. The INWISS prototype presented above has been built as a proof-of-concept for evaluating these proposals.

In chapter 5 we have proposed the use of semantic metadata (based on a hierarchical taxonomy as well as a more complex ontology) for content annotation. We have suggested text mining techniques for supporting the manual annotation process in a semi-automatic fashion in chapter 6. Based on the semantic metadata we apply a repository integration approach for global searching as presented in chapter 7 by consolidating metadata for intranet articles, external documents, as well as predefined OLAP reports in a single repository. Even though a real content management "service" (and the semi-automatic annotation) has not yet been implemented within our prototype, we use ontology-based metadata for searching. For this purpose we have implemented a similarity-based semantic search engine based on the proposal from chapter 8.

Building upon integration techniques (and in particular portlet standards) as discussed in chapter 9, the main contribution of this work is however the proposal for a context-based portlet integration in enterprise portals in chapter 10. The approach has been implemented within IN-WISS based on the Apache Jetspeed portal platform. As an example for an external application with access to structured database data we use a business intelligence system that views OLAP reports. The context-based portlet integration enables the portal to allow implicit searches for unstructured documents (based on their metadata) using the context of an OLAP report. The approach can, however, also be generalized to other scenarios. Another scenario that is implemented within the prototype is the integration of the content (management) portlet with a global taxonomy-based portal navigation.

The results are very promising. A major – although hardly measurable – success is the generic practicability of the context integration approach. The mentioned reporting portlet has been built completely independently, i.e. it contains no specific code that considers the existence of any of the other portlets. This ensures an applicability of the approach also for portlets that are provided as third party software components. The semantic search engine is only a byproduct of this main proposal. However, its evaluation is more tangible. Section 11.4.3 gives a first performance analysis. Although we still use generated test data and an imaginary company as a scenario, we can state that it achieves a significant gain in recall compared to approaches that do not consider semantic links within ontology-based metadata.

Chapter 12

Future Directions

In the previous chapter the the design of this work has been evaluated by presenting and evaluating its implementation in the INWISS knowledge portal prototype. As a remaining part of the evaluation phase of the research effort, this chapter shortly discusses suggestions for improvement that remain as future work.

The main contribution of this work was the proposal for a context-based portlet integration in enterprise portals in chapter 10. The approach has been implemented within the INWISS prototype (see chapter 11) based on the Apache Jetspeed portal platform and enables the portal to allow implicit searches for unstructured documents (based on their metadata) using the context of an OLAP report (representing structured data accessed through an application system). For this purpose a semantic search engine was implemented based on the proposal for a similarity-based information retrieval approach for ontology-based metadata from chapter 8. The prototype was intended as a proof-of-concept for the proposals made in this work, hence there is still room for improvement.

The first task that is subject to future work is the re-implementation of this search engine based on the Vector Space Model using the Lucene information retrieval framework[1] as a basis. This approach, which also allows a combination of metadata and fulltext-based searches, was already sketched in section 8.4. The integration of Lucene (and hence the availability of document vectors) opens up the possibility for implementing a content management component that supports a semi-automatic annotation as proposed in chapter 6.

Finally, as mentioned in chapter 10, in our context integration approach we so far only consider interaction context elements [HM03]. The first improvement in this area will be the addition of support for user context element, i.e. it will be possible to define a static context for each portal user (or role). The working context can be supported by integrating a workflow component into the portal as proposed in the following section.

12.1 Process-Orientation and Workflow

As already mentioned in chapter 3, an emerging trend in portal technology is process-orientation. Conventional portals are limited to giving existing applications a new look-and-feel and fulfilling visual preferences. Process portals guide users through business scenarios by organizing content and applications into automated business process flows [For04].

---

[1] http://jakarta.apache.org/lucene/

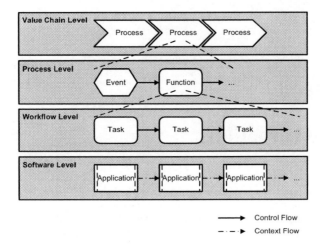

Figure 12.1: Supporting business processes through semantic context flow

Technically, process portals integrate workflow management functionality into portals in order to control the dialog flow from one application to the other. While existing process portal solutions can control the page flow from portlet to portlet, the transportation of the user context is still an unsolved issue. When a user moves from one application (e.g., CRM) to the other (e.g., order management), he/she will manually have to transport the information he/she works with (e.g., customer or stock item data). This problem can be addressed by extending the context integration approach from chapter 10.

The user context, represented using Semantic Web technologies, can be used as a link between the applications. While users move from application to application – ad-hoc or along the line of a pre-defined workflow – their context (e.g., the information about a certain customer) should follow along with them. When a user activates a task in the workflow task list the portal should move to a corresponding application portlet, providing the current user context to the target application. For example, the context from an "add customer" task, i.e. the information about a certain customer from the CRM system, can be taken as defaults for a "create account" task in the accounting system.

In our approach the context is so far volatile and bound to a user session. As an extension it can be bound to a workflow instance. This way the context will persist for the lifetime of the workflow instance and can even be transported from one user to the other if different responsibilities are defined. This idea of communicating the context among users of course raises security and privacy issues. However, it could be an interesting approach not only when embedded in a workflow. Also when using collaboration technology sending the context along with the user messages seems promising as the message can automatically be enriched with (and carry) the current context. The recipient can thus easily use the portal to find information related to the message received.

As discussed in chapter 6, a major issue in content management is the annotation of the documents with metadata. This metadata is particularly important for implicit, context-based searches. This metadata usually has to be created manually. Assume a quotation document is being created using a word processor. The user will use a CRM system to view the customer details and search an ERP system for product information and availability. If both systems are integrated into a context-aware portal system, the consolidated context (i.e. information about the customer and the products) can be used as a proposal for the metadata for the quotation document. Together with the text mining approach presented in chapter 6, this provides an extensive semi-automatic annotation facility.

In addition, the combination of workflow functionality with our context integration approach would allow us to also consider context elements that are modeled as part of a workflow task specification. Henrich & Morgenroth [HM03] call this the user's working context, comprising the role of the user in a business process, information relevant for the completion of the task, etc. A promising approach particularly suitable for the rather unstructured processes of knowledge work is presented in [HP05] based on the concept of knowledge stances.

12.2 Distribution

A further extension to the approach presented in this work is to use it in a distributed setting. Organizations could run a local instance of the portal and use it rather independently, however, the instances could cooperate using web service technology. Applications for such an approach would be distributed (or virtual) organizations, or collaborating organizations such as research institutes. There is currently a growing trend towards supporting distributed research collaboration under the umbrella of e-science and grid initiatives[2].

A distributed portal architecture is sketched in figure 12.2. Each portal instance would have its local content repository and set of application portlets and could hence run autonomously. In chapter 7 we presented two approaches for global searching, repository integration and meta searching. In a distributed scenario we propose to use a repository integration (indexing) approach for the local data sources, just like we do for our prototype (see chapter 11). In addition, if portal instances provide an externally accessible search interface, this interface can be used to also query remote instances and provide consolidated results by applying a meta search approach. In order to be able to access remote content, the content management service of a portal instance needs to provide a special interface as well. For read access it could simply be HTTP-based, for authoring functionality a WebDAV[3] or a web-service-based interface would be required.

As elaborated in chapter 9 portlets can be offered as remote portlets via Web Services for Remote Portlets (WSRP) [OAS03]. We have proposed extensions to the WSRP interfaces for our context-based portlet integration approach in chapter 10. Hence, also in a distributed setting portal instances can make the application functionality available as context-aware WSRP portlets.

The individual portal instances will use their own taxonomies and ontologies. These need to be integrated in order to support global searching, navigation, and context integration. For the ontology, ontological mapping as supported by the OWL ontology language can be applied, just like for the heterogeneous applications in a local setting (as proposed in chapters 7 and 10). For the taxonomy different approaches are possible. The taxonomy of a certain remote instance can be integrated as a sub-hierarchy into the local taxonomy for navigation. More sophisticated approaches could apply a topic mapping like for the ontology. Replication techniques could be used to make the integrated ontology available at all sites.

Finally, the registration and localization of the available instances (i.e. services) need to be accomplished. As we propose web-service-based interfaces UDDI registries [OAS02] could

---

[2]e.g., `http://www.nesc.ac.uk`, `http://www.d-grid.de`
[3]`http://www.ietf.org/html.charters/webdav-charter.html`

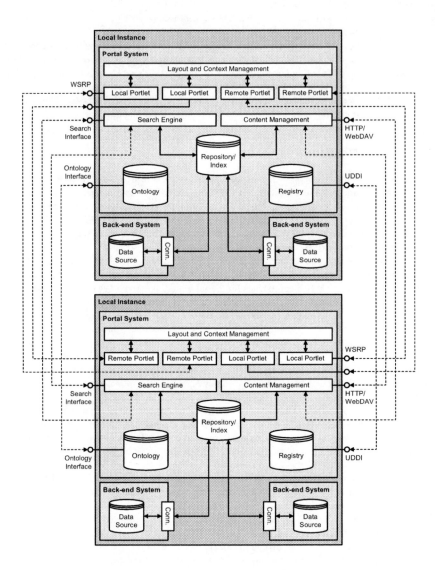

Figure 12.2: Distributed portal architecture

be used to provide a directory of available services (as also proposed for WSRP). Again, such registries could exist locally and use UDDI replication to share their information. Note that the (temporary) unavailability of certain remote instances (or individual services) would pose no problem for the local operability of a portal. It could still search its local sources and access its local applications.

Running cooperating portals in a distributed setting of course also opens up security issues. Users login into their local portal; their credentials are sent to the remote (search, content, or portlet) services along with the requests (single-sign-on). Credentials in this case usually mean the identity of the users, i.e. the individual instances need to know also the remote users and assign access privileges (or roles) to them. To avoid the need for registering the users at multiple sites a distributed (authentication and authorization) infrastructure could be utilized instead. Such so-called AAIs (e.g., Shibboleth[4]) [JL04] often use attributes for access control purposes in order to simplify the privilege administration. The CSAP security module [PMDP04] that we have integrated into our INWISS portal also supports an attribute-based access control model (ABAC) [PFMP04, PDMP05]. Introducing Semantic Web technologies also for mapping between different heterogeneous user attribute schemas is subject to future research.

---

[4]http://shibboleth.internet2.edu

Chapter 13

Conclusions

This chapter represents the *conclusion phase* of the design research effort presented
in this work by answering the research questions given in chapter 1, pointing to the
chapters that contribute to the answer.

Considering today's information society, efficient access to information of all kinds is becoming more and more important. Knowledge portals provide a means of addressing this issue within enterprises. In this work we have discussed how Semantic Web technologies can help building integrative enterprise knowledge portals that provide integrated and situational access to structured and unstructured information. Recall the research questions from chapter 1:

- *What are the requirements for providing an integrated, situational access to structured and unstructured information in enterprises?*
  In chapter 2 we have reviewed knowledge management literature and motivated integration and contextualization as the main requirements for efficient knowledge distribution. Integration means that we need to provide an integrated access to different information sources that exist within an enterprise. Contextualization refers to the fact that the information needs to be provided relevant to the user's current information need, i.e. aligned with its current business task.

- *Which are the (technical) features needed for this purpose?*
  Structured information is stored in databases and made accessible through (operational and analytical) applications; unstructured information is managed by content or document management. Their integration (and contextualization) is the main challenge for providing a situational information delivery. Hence, in the remainder of chapter 2 we have given a survey of related work on the integration of structured and unstructured information in knowledge management systems as well as on context-based information retrieval.

- *Which is the current (state-of-practice) solution of choice?*
  Enterprise knowledge portals provide means for integrating different information sources and applications within a single web-based user interface. Hence, they are the currently most promising base technology for our requirements. The architecture of enterprise knowledge portals as well as a survey of current portal solutions have been presented in chapter 3. Within enterprise knowledge portals, access to unstructured information is addressed by the content management base service. Application systems can be integrated by means of portlets. A further main portal component for our requirements is a

145

global search engine. Hence, content and structure management, global searching, and the integration of external applications are identified as major fields with potential for improvement.

- *Can content and structure management functionality be improved by using Semantic Web technologies?*
  After giving an overview on Semantic Web technologies in chapter 4, we have discussed the role of metadata and the potentials of using Semantic Web technologies in content and structure management in chapter 5. We conclude that the use of semantic metadata (based on an ontology) for content annotation promises a great improvement, in particular for searching. In addition, ontological mapping can help overcome heterogeneity issues of different data sources. However, the manual annotation of textual documents with metadata remains as a so far unsolved issue.

- *How can the annotation of documents with semantic metadata be accomplished?*
  In order to support the manual annotation of text documents, we have proposed a semi-automatic approach based on text mining and information extraction techniques in chapter 6. It turns out that text mining can be particularly helpful for linking documents with topics from a hierarchical taxonomy and elements from an ontology as proposed above.

- *Can global searching be improved by using Semantic Web technologies?*
  The main requirement for making (both structured and unstructured) information accessible for the users is searching. A global search facility constitutes a major component of a portal system. Techniques for global searching have been covered in chapter 7. We have discussed the use of ontology-based metadata and identified the need for a fuzzy search approach.

- *How can a fuzzy search on ontology-based metadata be realized?*
  As a solution for this issue we have presented an information retrieval approach for ontology-based metadata which provides fuzzy queries by utilizing the similarity of query and resource representations as known from IR models like the Vector Space Model (VSM) in chapter 8.

- *Can the integration of external applications into portals be improved by using Semantic Web technologies?*
  Techniques for integrating external applications into a portal by means of portlets have been presented in chapter 9. We conclude that third party portlets based on portlet standards such as the Java Portlet Specification or WSRP are the approach with the greatest potential. However, in today's portal systems there is only little interaction between those portlets. Existing inter-portlet communication capabilities are limited and unsuitable for third party (standard software) portlets as they do not address the semantics of the transmitted information. Again, Semantic Web technologies are promising for capturing those semantics and to overcome heterogeneity issues.

- *How can a generic, semantics-aware inter-portlet communication mechanism be realized in portal systems?*
  We have presented an approach for utilizing the user context for inter-portlet communication in chapter 10. We use Semantic Web technologies to capture the context and propose a context management service that is capable of supporting different (push and pull) communication scenarios.

In chapter 11 we have introduced our INWISS knowledge portal prototype which is used as a proof-of-concept to evaluate the above proposals. The results are very promising: The context-based portlet integration approach shows generic applicability, also for portlets that are provided as third party software components; the semantic search engine achieves a significant gain in recall compared to approaches that do not consider semantic links within ontology-based metadata. Nevertheless, we still use an imaginary company as a scenario. A truly empirical evaluation was so far not possible, but we are currently trying to acquire funds to implement the prototype as a pilot system in a real enterprise setting.

As elaborated in chapter 12, additional future work will involve the integration of workflow functionality in order to apply our context integration also to process portals as well as the applicability of our approach in a distributed setting, e.g., for e-science scenarios. Furthermore, in another project we are working on utilizing user attributes and resource metadata for access control purposes. A security module with an attribute-based access control facility [PMDP04] has already been integrated into the INWISS prototype. An interesting next step will be to use the user attributes (e.g., his location) also as context elements for our context-based portlet integration.

Appendix A

Additional Material

A.1 Ontology of the Scenario

Figure A.1 on the following page shows a UML diagram of the ontology used as a scenario for our prototype; it was derived from the VMall demo data set provided with the business intelligence system MicroStrategy 7i[1] that is used by our reporting portlet (see chapter 11). Note that only the classes and their properties are shown. Instances of the Object class (and its subclasses) are used for the annotation of resources (and for search queries) via dc:coverage; instances of the Author class are used as potential creators of resources and assigned with dc:creator.

---

[1]http://www.microstrategy.com

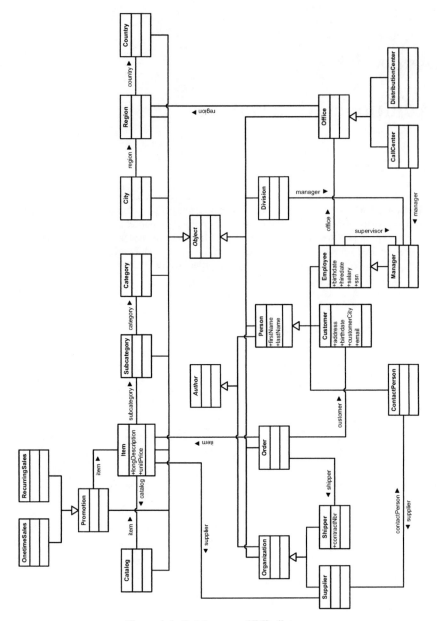

Figure A.1: Ontology as a UML diagram

A.2 Evaluation Queries

The following sample queries have been used to evaluate the semantic search engine presented in chapter 11, which is based on the similarity-based information retrieval approach for ontology-based metadata from chapter 8. Queries1 through Query5 (figure A.2) are handcrafted user queries, Query6 through Query10 (figure A.3) are context-based "find related" queries.

```
@prefix dc:    <http://purl.org/dc/elements/1.1/>
@prefix onto:  <http://www.inwiss.org/ontology#>
@prefix :      <http://www.inwiss.org/evaluation/>

:Query1 dc:title "*fall*" .
:Query1 dc:title "*brochure*" .

:Query2 dc:description "*supply*" .
:Query2 dc:description "*contract*" .
:Query2 dc:coverage onto:Audio .

:Query3 dc:coverage onto:Gadgets .

:Query4 dc:title "*brochure*" .
:Query4 dc:description "*espresso*" .
:Query4 dc:format "application/msword" .

:Query5 dc:title "*brochure*" .
:Query5 dc:coverage onto:SkinCare .
```

Figure A.2: Evaluation queries 1-13 in N3 notation

For Query9 and Query10 in figure A.3 on the following page note that within the ontology mstr:element is mapped to be an owl:equivalentProperty of dc:coverage and OLAP elements are mapped to be owl:sameAs the corresponding ontology objects (e.g. http://www.microstrategy.com/elements/Subcategory_1 is identical with onto:Electronics). The same applies to mstr:folder and the folder instances.

```
@prefix dc:   <http://purl.org/dc/elements/1.1/>
@prefix onto:   <http://www.inwiss.org/ontology#>
@prefix mstr:   <http://www.microstrategy.com/terms/>
@prefix :   <http://www.inwiss.org/evaluation/>

:Query6 dc:subject
  <http://www.inwiss.org/topics/Marketing/Electronics/Gadgets> .
:Query6 dc:coverage onto:KeytogLaserPointer .

:Query7 dc:subject <http://www.inwiss.org/topics/Sales> .
:Query7 dc:coverage onto:Electronics .

:Query8 dc:subject
  <http://www.inwiss.org/topics/Marketing/HealthBeauty/SkinCare> .
:Query8 dc:coverage onto:LuxuriousBathPack .

:Query9 mstr:folder <http://www.microstrategy.com/folders/Sales> .
:Query9 mstr:metric <http://www.microstrategy.com/metrics/DollarSales> .
:Query9 mstr:element
  <http://www.microstrategy.com/elements/Quarter_199801> .
:Query9 mstr:element
  <http://www.microstrategy.com/elements/Quarter_199802> .
:Query9 mstr:element
  <http://www.microstrategy.com/elements/Quarter_199803> .
:Query9 mstr:element
  <http://www.microstrategy.com/elements/Quarter_199804> .
:Query9 mstr:element
  <http://www.microstrategy.com/elements/Subcategory_1> .
:Query9 mstr:element
  <http://www.microstrategy.com/elements/Subcategory_7> .
:Query9 mstr:element
  <http://www.microstrategy.com/elements/Subcategory_9> .

:Query10 mstr:folder <http://www.microstrategy.com/folders/Sales> .
:Query10 mstr:metric <http://www.microstrategy.com/metrics/DollarSales> .
:Query10 mstr:element
  <http://www.microstrategy.com/elements/Quarter_199801> .
:Query10 mstr:element
  <http://www.microstrategy.com/elements/Quarter_199802> .
:Query10 mstr:element
  <http://www.microstrategy.com/elements/Quarter_199803> .
:Query10 mstr:element
  <http://www.microstrategy.com/elements/Quarter_199804> .
:Query10 mstr:element <http://www.microstrategy.com/elements/Item_83> .
:Query10 mstr:element <http://www.microstrategy.com/elements/Item_131> .
:Query10 mstr:element <http://www.microstrategy.com/elements/Item_172> .
```

Figure A.3: Evaluation queries 14 and 15 in N3 notation

Bibliography

[ABM⁺00]   A. Abecker, A. Bernardi, H. Maus, M. Sintek, and C. Wenzel. Information Supply for Business Processes: Coupling Workflow with Document Analysis and Information Retrieval. *Knowledge Based Systems*, 13(5):271–284, 2000.

[ABN⁺01]   A. Abecker, A. Bernardi, S. Ntioudis, R. Herterich, C. Houy, M. Legal, G. Mentzas, and S. Müller. The DECOR Toolbox for Workflow-Embedded Organizational Memory Access. In *Proc. of the 3rd International Conference on Enterprise Information Systems (ICEIS 2001)*, Setubal, Portugal, July 2001.

[Apa04]   The Jetspeed Portal Tutorial 1.5. Apache Software Foundation, 2004. http://portals.apache.org/jetspeed-1/tutorial/. Retrieved May 9, 2005.

[Aud02]   S. Audersch. XML-basiertes Content-Management mit OLAP-Funktionalität auf der Basis von RDF. Presentation at the workshop of the GI working group "Konzepte des Data Warehousing", Munich, Germany, March 2002.

[Aug90]   S. Augustin. *Information als Wettbewerbsfaktor. Informationslogistik – Herausforderungen an das Management*. Verlag Industrielle Organisation Zürich, 1990.

[Bar03]   A. Baron. A Developer's Introduction to Web Parts, May 2003. http://msdn.microsoft.com/library/default.asp?url=/library/en-us/odc_sp2003_ta/html/sharepoint_northwindwebparts.asp. Retrieved May 9, 2005.

[BE97]   R. Barzilay and M. Elhadad. Using Lexical Chains for Text Summarization. In *Proceedings of the ACL'97/EACL'97 Workshop on Intelligent Scalable Text Summarization*, Madrid, Spain, 1997.

[BH00]   J. Budzik and K. Hammond. User Interactions with Everyday Applications as Context for Just-in-Time Information Access. In *Proc. of the 2000 International Conferece on Intelligent User Interfaces*, New Orleans, LA, USA, 2000. ACM Press.

[BH05]   K. Böhm and J. Härtwig. Prozessorientiertes Wissensmanagement durch kontextualisierte Informationsversorgung aus Geschäftsprozessen. In *Proc. 6. Internationale Tagung Wirtschaftsinformatik (WI 2005)*, pp. 943–962, Bamberg, Germany, February 2005.

[BKvH02]   J. Broekstra, A. Kampman, and F. van Harmelen. Sesame: A Generic Architecture for Storing and Querying RDF and RDF Schema. In *Proc. of the First International Semantic Web Conference (ISWC 2002)*, Sardinia, Italy, June 2002.

[BL98]   T. Berners-Lee.   A Roadmap to the Semantic Web.   World Wide Web
            Consortium, September 1998. http://www.w3.org/DesignIssues/
            Semantic.html. Retrieved May 9, 2005.

[BL00]   T. Berners-Lee. Semantic Web on XML. Keynote session at XML 2000, Wash-
            ington, DC, USA, December 2000.

[BL02]   R. Bellaver and J. Lusa. *Knowledge Management Strategy and Technology.*
            Artech House, 2002.

[BLC03]   T. Berners-Lee and D. Connolly.   Primer: Getting into RDF & Se-
            mantic Web using N3.   World Wide Web Consortium,   April 2003.
            http://www.w3.org/2000/10/swap/Primer.html. Retrieved May
            9, 2005.

[BLHL01]   T. Berners-Lee, J. Hendler, and O. Lassila. The Semantic Web. *Scientific Amer-
            ican*, May 2001.

[BMR+96]   F. Buschmann, R. Meunier, H. Rohnert, P. Sommerlad, and M. Stal. *Pattern-
            Oriented Software Architecture: A System of Patterns.* John Wiley & Sons, 1996.

[Bow]   L. Bowden.   Portal Solutions.   IBM Corporation.   http://www-
            306.ibm.com/software/info1/websphere/index.jsp?tab=
            videoqa/index&vid=bowden. Retrieved May 9, 2005.

[Bs99]   V. Bach and H. Österle. Wissensmanagement: Eine unternehmerische Perspek-
            tive. In V. Bach, H. Österle, and P. Vogler (Eds.), *Business Knowledge Manage-
            ment in der Praxis*, pp. 13–35. Springer, Berlin et al., 1999.

[BYRN99]   R. Baeza-Yates and B. Ribeiro-Neto (Eds.). *Modern Information Retrieval.* Ad-
            dison Wesley Longman Limited, Essex, 1999.

[Car02]   J. Carroll. Matching RDF Graphs. In *Proc. of the First International Semantic
            Web Conference (ISWC 2002)*, pp. 5–15, Sardinia, Italy, June 2002.

[Car03a]   J. Carbonell. Grand Challenges for Information Management. In *Proc. Twelfth
            International Conference on Information and Knowledge Management (CIKM
            2003)*, New Orleans, LA, USA, November 2003.

[Car03b]   J. Carroll. Signing RDF Graphs. In *Proc. of the Second International Semantic
            Web Conference (ISWC 2003)*, Sansibel Island, FL, USA, October 2003.

[CD97]   S. Chaudhuri and U. Dayal.   An Overview of Data Warehousing and OLAP
            Technology. *ACM SIGMOD Record*, 26(1), March 1997.

[CGPLC+03] O. Corcho, A. Gomez-Perez, A. Lopez-Cima, V. Lopez-Garcia, and
            M. d. C. Suarez-Figueroa. ODESeW – Automatic Generation of Knowledge
            Portals for Intranets and Extranets. In *Proc. of the 2nd International Semantic
            Web Conference (ISWC 2003)*, Sansibel Island, FL, USA, 2003.

[CK67]   C. A. Cuadra and R. V. Katter. Opening the Black Box of Relevance. *Journal of
            Documentation*, (23):291–303, 1967.

[CM04]   T. Choo and M. Moore. WebSphere Portal and Microsoft SharePoint Integration Guide, 2004. `http://www-128.ibm.com/developerworks/ websphere/library/techarticles/0410_choo/0410_choo .html`. Retrieved May 9, 2005.

[CMK66]   C. Cleverdon, J. Mills, and M. Keen. Factors Determining the Performance of Indexing Systems. Volume 1: Design. ASLIB Cranfield Research Project, 1966.

[Col03]   H. Collins. *Enterprise Knowledge Portals.* AMACOM American Management Association, New York et al., 2003.

[Cre94]   J. W. Creswell. *Research Design: Qualitative & Quantitative Approaches.* SAGE Publications, 1994.

[DA99]   A. K. Dey and G. D. Abowd. Towards a Better Understanding of Context and Context-Awareness. College of Computing, Georgia Institute of Technology (No. GIT-GVU-99-32), Atlanta, GA, USA, 1999.

[DAM03]   SWRL: A Semantic Web Rule Language Combining OWL and RuleML. Joint US/EU ad hoc Agent Markup Language Committee, November 2003. `http://www.daml.org/2003/11/swrl/`. Retrieved May 9, 2005.

[Dav01]   M. M. Davydov. *Corporate Portals and e-Business Integration.* McGraw-Hill, New York, 2001.

[DB94]   S. Davis and J. Botkin. The Coming of Knowledge-Based Business. *Harvard Business Review*, pp. 165–170, September/October 1994.

[DCM02]   Expressing Qualified Dublin Core in RDF/XML. Dublin Core Metadata Initiative, May 2002. `http://dublincore.org/documents/ 2002/05/15/dcq-rdf-xml/`. Retrieved May 9, 2005.

[DCM03]   DCMI Metadata Terms. Dublin Core Metadata Initiative, November 2003. `http://dublincore.org/documents/2003/11/19/ dcmi-terms/`. Retrieved May 9, 2005.

[DEFS99]   S. Decker, M. Erdmann, D. Fensel, and R. Studer. Ontobroker: Ontology Based Access to Distributed and Semi-Structured Information. In R. Meersman et al. (Eds.), *Database Semantics: Semantic Issues in Multimedia Systems*, pp. 351–369. Kluwer Academic Publishers, 1999.

[DeW02]   S. DeWitt. Basic Web Clipping Using WebSphere Portal Version 4.1. IBM Corporation, 2002. `http://www-106.ibm.com/developerworks/ websphere/library/techarticles/0206_dewitt/dewitt .html`. Retrieved May 9, 2005.

[DJB96]   T. H. Davenport, S. Jarvenpaa, and M. Beers. Improving Knowledge Work Processes. *Sloan Management Review*, 37(4):53–65, 1996.

[Dow03]   A. Dowler. Integration Guide for Microsoft Office 2003 and Windows SharePoint Services, June 2003. `http://www.microsoft.com/ technet/prodtechnol/windowsserver2003/technologies/ sharepoint/spoffint.mspx`. Retrieved May 9, 2005.

[DP98]   T. H. Davenport and L. Prusak. *Working Knowledge: How Organizations Manage What They Know.* Harvard Business School Press, Boston, 1998.

[Ehl02]   L. Ehlers. *Content Management Anwendungen – Spezifikation von Internet-Anwendungen auf Basis von Content Management Systemen.* Logos, Berlin, 2002.

[EK03]   J. S. Edwards and J. B. Kidd. Bridging the Gap from the General to the Specific by Linking Knowledge Management to Business Processes. In V. Hlupic (Ed.), *Knowledge and Business Process Management*, pp. 118–136. Idea Group Publishing, Hershey, 2003.

[Eri04]   J. Ericson. Microsoft Toolkits for Portals. PortalsMag.com News, August 2004. http://www.portalsmag.com/articles/default.asp? ArticleID=5865&TopicID=7. Retrieved May 9, 2005.

[Fel01]   R. Feldman. Mining Unstructured Data. Tutorial at the Tenth International Conference on Information and Knowledge Management (CIKM 2001), Atlanta, GA, USA, November 2001.

[Fen01]   D. Fensel. *Ontologies: A Silver Bullet for Knowledge Management and Electronic Commerce.* Springer, 2001.

[Fen02]   K. Fenstermacher. Process-Aware Knowledge Retrieval. In *Proc. of the 35th Annual Hawaii International Conference on System Science (HICSS 2002)*, volume 7, p. 209ff, Hawaii, 2002.

[Fer03]   R. Ferber. *Information Retrieval – Suchmodelle und Data-Mining-Verfahren für Textsammlungen und das Web.* dpunkt.verlag, Heidelberg, 2003.

[FG02]   R. Franken and A. Gadatsch. *Integriertes Knowledge Management.* Vieweg & Sohn, 2002.

[FK01]   F. Fuchs-Kittowski. Wissens-Ko-Produktion und dynamische Netze: Kooperative Wissenserzeugung und -nutzung in wissensintensiven Geschäftsprozessen. In H. J. Müller, A. Abecker, and H. Maus (Eds.), *Proc. of the Workshop Prozessorientiertes Wissensmanagement, 1. Konferenz Professionelles Wissensmanagement (WM 2001)*, Baden-Baden, Germany, 2001.

[FK02]   G. Färber and J. Kirchner. *mySAP Technology.* Galileo Press, Bonn, 2002.

[For04]   Process Portal Platforms. Forrester Research, 2004. http://www.forrester.com/TechRankings/CategoryMain/1,5821,48,00.html. Retrieved May 9, 2005.

[Ger02]   R. Gersdorf. Potenziale des Content-Management. *Wirtschaftsinformatik*, 44(2), 2002.

[GH03]   T. Gurzki and H. Hinderer. Eine Referenzarchitektur für Software zur Realisierung von Unternehmensportalen. In *2. Konferenz Professionelles Wissensmanagement (WM 2003)*, Lucerne, Switzerland, 2003.

[GHE02]   T. Gurzki, H. Hinderer, and C.-T. Eberhard. Marktübersicht Portal Software
           für Business-, Enterprise-Portale und E-Collaboration. Fraunhofer IRB Verlag,
           2002.

[GN00]   G. Grefenstette and J. Nioche. The WWW as a Resource for Lexicography.
           In M.-H. Corréard (Ed.), *Lexicography and Natural Language Processing*, pp.
           199–215. 2000.

[GR04]   A. Goebel and D. Ritthaler. *SAP Enterprise Portal*. Galileo Press, Bonn, 2004.

[Gru93]   T. Gruber. A Translation Approach to Portable Ontology Specifications. *Knowl-
           edge Acquisition*, (5):199–220, 1993.

[Gur03]   A. Guruge. *Corporate Portals - Empowered with XML and Web Services*. Digital
           Press, 2003.

[Ham03]   B. Hammersley. *Content Syndication with RSS*. O'Reilly & Associates, Beijing,
           2003.

[HBH⁺98]   E. Horvitz, J. Breese, D. Heckerman, D. Hovel, and K. Rommelse. The Lumìere
           Project: Bayesian User Modeling for Inferring the Goals and Needs of Software
           Users. In *Proc. of the 14th Conf. on Uncertainty in Artificial Intelligence*, pp.
           256–265, Madison, WI, USA, July 1998.

[Hei01]   P. Heisig. Business Process Oriented Knowledge Management. In K. Mertins,
           P. Heisig, and J. Vorbeck (Eds.), *Knowledge Management – Best Practices in
           Europe*, pp. 14–36. Springer, Berlin, 2001.

[Hep03]   S. Hepper. Comparing the JSR 168 Java Portlet Specification with the
           IBM Portlet API. IBM Corporation, December 2003. `http://www-
           106.ibm.com/developerworks/websphere/library/
           techarticles/0312_hepper/hepper.html`. Retrieved May 9,
           2005.

[HHL02]   J. Heflin, J. Hendler, and S. Luke. SHOE: A Blueprint for the Semantic Web.
           In D. Fensel, J. Hendler, H. Lieberman, and W. Wahlster (Eds.), *Spinning the
           Semantic Web: Bringing the World Wide Web to Its Full Potential*. MIT Press,
           2002.

[Hig05]   J. Higgins. Homographs: A List of English Words Which Have Two
           Pronunciations But One Spelling. Stirling, 2005. `http://www.
           marlodge.supanet.com/wordlist/homogrph.html`. Retrieved
           May 9, 2005.

[HM02]   A. Henrich and K. Morgenroth. Integration von kontextunterstütztem Informa-
           tion Retrieval in Portalsysteme. In *Teilkonferenz Management der Mitarbeiter-
           Expertise in IT-Beratungsunternehmen, MKWI 2002*, Nürnberg, Germany, 2002.

[HM03]   A. Henrich and K. Morgenroth. Supporting Collaborative Software Develop-
           ment by Context-Aware Information Retrieval Facilities. In *Proc. of the DEXA
           2003 Workshop on Web Based Collaboration (WBC 2003)*, Prague, Czech Re-
           public, September 2003.

[HP05]   T. Hädrich and T. Priebe. Supporting Knowledge Work with Knowledge-Stance-
            Oriented Integrative Portals. In *Proc. of the13th European Conference on Infor-
            mation Systems (ECIS 2005)*, Regensburg, Germany, May 2005.

[HSC02]   S. Handschuh, S. Staab, and F. Ciravegna. S-CREAM – Semi-automatic CRE-
            Ation of Metadata. In *Proc. of the European Conference on Knowledge Acqui-
            sition and Management (EKAW 2002)*, Madrid, Spain, October 2002.

[IBM]   Using JSR 168 with WebSphere Portal. IBM Corporation. http://publib.
            boulder.ibm.com/pvc/wp/5021/ent/en/standards/jsr168
            .html. Retrieved May 9, 2005.

[JCP03]   Java Servlet Specification Version 2.4.   Java Community Process,
            2003.   http://jcp.org/aboutJava/communityprocess/final/
            jsr154/index.html. Retrieved May 9, 2005.

[JCP04]   Java Portlet Specification Version 1.0.   Java Community Process, 2004.
            http://jcp.org/aboutJava/communityprocess/final/
            jsr168/index.html. Retrieved May 9, 2005.

[JFM97]   T. Joachims, D. Freitag, and T. M. Mitchell. Web Watcher: A Tour Guide for
            the World Wide Web. In *Proc. of the 15th International Joint Conference on
            Artificial Intelligence (IJCAI 1997)*, pp. 770–777, 1997.

[JL04]   G. P. J. Lopez, R. Opplieger. Authentication and Authorization Infrastructures
            (AAIs): A Comparative Survey. *Computers & Security*, 23(7):578–590, 2004.

[KB04]   C. Kiss and M. Bichler.   Data Mining and Campaign Management in the
            Telecommunications Industry. In *Coordination and Agent Technology in Value
            Networks (MKWI 2004)*. GITO-Verlag, 2004.

[Kel03]   G. H. Kelman. Plumtree Ships Products to Fully Support WSRP and Pro-
            posed JSR 168 Portlet Standards.   Plumtree Software, September 2003.
            http://portal.plumtree.com/portal/server.pt/gateway/
            PTARGS_0_661205_550908_0_0_18/Sept%203,%202003%20
            Press%20Release-%20%20Plumtree%20Releases%20WSRP%20
            and%20JSR%20168%20Products.doc. Retrieved May 9, 2005.

[Kel04]   G. H. Kelman.   Plumtree Software's Developer Support – Build-
            ing Applications on the Enterprise Web.   Plumtree Software, 2004.
            http://portal.plumtree.com/portal/server.pt/gateway/
            PTARGS_0_661205_588994_0_0_18/Q1%202004%20White%20
            Paper%20on%20Plumtree's%20Developer%20Support.doc.
            Retrieved May 9, 2005.

[KJvO01]   J. Koop, K. Jäckel, and A. van Offern. *Erfolgsfaktor Content Management*.
            Vieweg & Sohn, 2001.

[Kle00]   R. Klemke. Context Framework – An Open Approach to Enhance Organizational
            Memory Systems with Context Modeling Techniques. In *Proc. of the Third In-
            ternational Conference on Practical Aspects of Knowledge Management (PAKM
            2000)*, Basel, Switzerland, October 2000.

[KLM96]   L. P. Kaelbling, M. L. Littman, and A. W. Moore. Reinforcement Learning: A Survey. *Journal of Artificial Intelligence Research*, (4):237–285, 1996.

[KM04]   G. Kelman and J. McVeigh. Plumtree Software: 1997-2004 Our Products, Our Vision, 2004. http://www.plumtree.com/moreinfo/. Retrieved May 9, 2005.

[KMM00]   Z. Kouba, K. Matousek, and P. Miksovsky. On Data Warehouse and GIS Integration. In *Proc. 11th International Conference on Database and Expert Systems Applications (DEXA 2000)*, Greenwich, UK, September 2000.

[KP97]   J. Küng and J. Palkoska. VQS – A Vague Query System Prototype. In *Proc. of the 8th International Workshop on Database and Expert Systems Applications (DEXA 1997), W9: Special Databases*, Toulouse, France, 1997.

[KQPW03]   A. Kao, L. Quach, S. Poteet, and S. Woods. User Assisted Text Classification and Knowledge Management. In *Proc. of the Twelfth International Conference on Information and Knowledge Management (CIKM 2004)*, New Orleans, LA, USA, November 2003.

[Leh00]   F. Lehner. *Organizational Memory Systems*. Carl Hanser Verlag, Munich, Germany, 2000.

[Lie97]   H. Lieberman. Autonomous Interface Agents. In *Proceedings of the ACM Conference on Computers and Human Interface (CHI 1997)*, Atlanta, GA, USA, 1997.

[LR02]   D. B. Lection and V. Ramamoorthy. Websphere Portal V4 Programming, Part 2: Portlet Application Programming. IBM Corporation, August 2002. http://www-106.ibm.com/developerworks/ibm/library/i-portal2v4/. Retrieved May 9, 2005.

[Mac04]   L. MacVittie. Enterprise Portals Suites – Portal Power. 2004. http://www.networkcomputing.com/showitem.jhtml?articleID=18900467&pgno=4. Retrieved May 9, 2005.

[Mae02]   A. Maedche. *Ontology Learning For The Semantic Web*. Kluwer Academic Publishers, 2002.

[Mai04]   R. Maier. *Knowledge Management Systems: Information and Communication Technologies for Knowledge Management*. Springer, Berlin et al., 2004.

[Mau01]   H. Maus. Workflow Context as a Means for Intelligent Information Support. In *Proc. of 3rd Intl. Conf. on Modeling and Using Context (CONTEXT 2001)*, pp. 261–274, 2001.

[McG02]   D. McGuinness. Ontologies Come of Age. In D. Fensel, J. Hendler, H. Lieberman, and W. Wahlster (Eds.), *Spinning the Semantic Web: Bringing the World Wide Web to Its Full Potential*. MIT Press, 2002.

[MHSV04]   E. Mäkelä, E. Hyvönen, S. Saarela, and K. Viljanen. OntoViews – A Tool for Creating Semantic Web Portals. In *Proc. of the 3rd International Semantic Web Conference (ISWC 2004)*, Hiroshima, Japan, 2004.

[MMP99]   J. Mayeld, P. McNamee, and C. Piatko. The JHU/APL HAIRCUT System at
            TREC-8. In *The Eighth Text Retrieval Conference (TREC-8)*, pp. 445–452,
            Gaithersburg, Maryland, USA, November 1999.

[MR03]   R. Maier and U. Remus. Implementing Process-oriented Knowledge Manage-
            ment Strategies. *Journal of Knowledge Management*, 7(4):62–74, 2003.

[MS02]   R. Maier and J. Sametinger. Infotop – An Information and Communication In-
            frastructure for Knowledge Work. In *Proc. of the 3rd European Conference on
            Knowledge Management*, Dublin, Ireland, 2002.

[MS04]   D. Marshak and P. Seybold. An Executive's Guide to Portals: What Customer-
            Centric Executives Need to Know about Portals. Patricia Seybold Group,
            2004. http://www.psgroup.com/vm/portals/report.asp. Re-
            trieved May 9, 2005.

[MST94]   D. Michie, D. Spiegelhalter, and C. Taylor. *Machine Learning, Neural and Sta-
            tistical Classification*. Ellis Horwood, New York, 1994.

[Mye97]   M. Myers. Qualitative Research in Information Systems. *MIS Quarterly*,
            21(2):241–242, June 1997. http://www.qual.auckland.ac.nz. Re-
            trieved May 9, 2005.

[MYL02]   W. Meng, C. Yu, and K.-L. Liu. Building Efficient and Effective Metasearch
            Engines. *ACM Computing Surveys*, 34(1):48–89, 2002.

[Nai82]   J. Naisbitt. *Megatrends: Ten New Directions Transforming Our Lives*. Warner
            Books, 1982.

[NT95]   I. Nonaka and H. Takehuchi. *The Knowledge-Creating Company*. Oxford Uni-
            versity Press, Oxford et al., 1995.

[Nur98]   R. Nurmi. Knowledge-Intensive Firms. *Business Horizons*, 41(3):26–32, 1998.

[OAS02]   UDDI Version 3.0 Specification. OASIS, July 2002. http://uddi.org/
            pubs/uddi-v3.00-published-20020719.pdf. Retrieved May 9,
            2005.

[OAS03]   Web Services for Remote Portlets Specification. OASIS, August 2003.
            http://www.oasis-open.org/committees/download.php/
            3343/oasis-200304-wsrp-specification-1.0.pdf. Retrieved
            May 9, 2005.

[OI01]   W. Orlikowski and C. Iacono. Desperately Seeking the "IT" in IT Research –
            A Call to Theorizing the IT Artifact. *Information Systems Research*, 12(2):121–
            134, 2001.

[PB03]   J. Paralic and P. Bednar. Text Mining for Document Annotation and Ontology
            Support. In *Intelligent Systems at the Service of Mankind*, pp. 237–248. Ubooks,
            2003.

[PDMP05]   T. Priebe, W. Dobmeier, B. Muschall, and G. Pernul. ABAC – Ein Referenzmod-
            ell für attributbasierte Zugriffskontrolle. In *Proc. 2. Jahrestagung Fachbereich
            Sicherheit der Gesellschaft für Informatik (Sicherheit 2005)*, Regensburg, Ger-
            many, April 2005.

[PFMP04]   T. Priebe, E. B. Fernandez, J. I. Mehlau, and G. Pernul. A Pattern System for
             Access Control. In *Proc. 18th Annual IFIP WG 11.3 Working Conference on
             Data and Application Security*, Sitges, Spain, July 2004.

[Pie31]   C. S. Pierce. *Collected Papers*. Harvard University Press, Cambridge, MA,
             1931.

[PKK05]   T. Priebe, C. Kiss, and J. Kolter. Semiautomatische Annotation von Textdoku-
             menten mit semantischen Metadaten. In *Proc. 6. Internationale Tagung
             Wirtschaftsinformatik (WI 2005)*, Bamberg, Germany, February 2005.

[PMDP04]   T. Priebe, B. Muschall, W. Dobmeier, and G. Pernul. A Flexible Security System
             for Enterprise and e-Government Portals. In *Proc. of the 15th International Con-
             ference on Database and Expert Systems Applications (DEXA 2004)*, Zaragoza,
             Spain, September 2004.

[Pop02]   K. Popp. Nutzbarmachung von Portaltechnologie: mySAP Enterprise Portals.
             In S. Meinhardt and K. Popp (Eds.), *Enterprise-Portale & Enterprise Appli-
             cation Integration (HMD 225)*, Praxis der Wirtschaftsinformatik, pp. 21–29.
             dpunkt.verlag, Heidelberg, Germany, June 2002.

[Por85]   M. Porter. *Competitive Advantage: Creating and Sustaining Superior Perfor-
             mance*. Free Press, New York, 1985.

[PP03]   T. Priebe and G. Pernul. Towards Integrative Enterprise Knowledge Portals. In
             *Proc. Twelfth International Conference on Information and Knowledge Manage-
             ment (CIKM 2003)*, New Orleans, LA, USA, November 2003.

[Pri04]   T. Priebe. INWISS – Integrative Enterprise Knowledge Portal. Demonstration
             at the 3rd International Semantic Web Conference (ISWC 2004), Hiroshima,
             Japan, 2004.

[PRR99]   G. Probst, S. Raub, and K. Romhardt. *Managing Knowledge: Building Blocks
             for Success*. Wiley & Sons, West Sussex, 1999.

[Qui86]   J. R. Quinlan. Induction of Decision Trees. *Machine Learning*, 1(1), 1986.

[Raj01]   R. Rajkumar. *Industrial Knowledge Management: A Micro Level Approach*.
             Springer, 2001.

[RC03]   A. Roy-Chowdhury.   Using Cooperative Portlets in WebSphere Portal
             V5.   IBM Corporation, October 2003.   http://www-106.ibm.com/
             developerworks/websphere/library/techarticles/0310_
             roy/roy.html. Retrieved May 9, 2005.

[Rho00]   B. J. Rhodes. *Just-In-Time Information Retrieval*. Phd thesis, MIT Media Labo-
             ratory, Cambridge, MA, May 2000.

[RKvM00]   B. Rieger, A. Kleber, and E. von Maur. Metadata-based Integration of Qualitative
             and Quantitative Information Resources Approaching Knowledge Management.
             In *Proc. 8th European Conference of Information Systems*, Vienna, Austria, July
             2000.

[SAP02]   Administration Guide Portal Platform – Enterprise Portal 5.0. SAP AG, 2002.
             http://help.sap.com/saphelp_ep50sp6/helpdata/en/start
             .htm. Retrieved May 9, 2005.

[SAP03]   Repository   Framework   Concepts.   SAP   AG,   August   2003.
             https://www.sdn.sap.com/irj/servlet/prt/portal/
             prtroot/com.sapportals.km.docs/documents/a1-8-4/
             Repository%20Framework%20Concepts. Retrieved May 9, 2005.

[SDW01]   T. Scheffler, C. Decomain, and S. Wrobel. Active Hidden Markov Models for
             Information Extraction. In *International Symposium on Intelligent Data Analysis
             (IDA)*, 2001.

[SE97]   E. Selberg and O. Etzioni. The MetaCrawler Architecture for Resource Aggre-
             gation on the Web. *IEEE Expert*, 12(1), 1997.

[Seb02]   F. Sebastiani. Machine Learning in Automated Text Categorization. *ACM Com-
             puting Surveys*, 34(1), 2002.

[SFJ+02]   U. Shah, T. Finin, A. Joshi, R. Cost, and J. Mayfield. Information Retrieval
             On The Semantic Web. In *Proc. of the Eleventh International Conference on
             Information and Knowledge Management (CIKM 2002)*. McLean, VA, USA,
             November 2002.

[SGB04]   D. Straub,   D. Gefen,   and M.-C. Boudreau.   Quantitative,
             Positivist Research Methods in Information Systems, 2004.
             http://www.dstraub.cis.gsu.edu:88/quant/. Retrieved May 9,
             2005.

[SH01]   A. Swartz and J. Hendler. The Semantic Web: A Network of Content for the
             Digital City. In *Proc. of the Second Annual Digital Cities Workshop*, Kyoto,
             Japan, October 2001.

[SMS+01]   N. Stojanovic, A. Maedche, S. Staab, R. Studer, and Y. Sure. SEAL – A Frame-
             work for Developing SEmantic PortALs. In *Proc. of the First International Con-
             ference on Knowledge Capture (K-CAP 2001)*, Victoria, BC, Canada, October
             2001.

[ST03]   T. Schaeck and R. Thompson. Web Services for Remote Portlets (WSRP)
             Whitepaper.   OASIS, 2003.   http://www.oasis-open.org/
             committees/download.php/2634/WSRP%20Whitepaper%20-%20
             rev%202.doc. Retrieved May 9, 2005.

[Sto03]   N. Stojanovic. An Explanation-Based Ranking Approach for Ontology-Based
             Querying. In *Proc. International Conference on Database and Expert Systems
             (DEXA 2003)*, Prague, Czech Republic, September 2003.

[SW02]   J. Schelp and R. Winter. Enterprise Portals und Enterprise Application Inte-
             gration – Begriffsbestimmung und Integrationskonzeption. In S. Meinhardt and
             K. Popp (Eds.), *Enterprise-Portale & Enterprise Application Integration (HMD
             225)*, Praxis der Wirtschaftsinformatik, pp. 6–20. dpunkt.verlag, Heidelberg,
             Germany, June 2002.

[Tan99]   A. Tan. *Text Mining: The State of the Art and the Challenges*. Kent Ridge Digital Labs, Singapore, 1999.

[TKL⁺03]   F. Theis, S. Kuhn, M. Langham, J. Müller, D. Wang, and C. Ziegler. *Portale und Webapplikatinen mit Apache Frameworks*. Software & Support, Frankfurt, 2003.

[TVTY90]   H. Takeda, P. Veerkamp, T. Tomiyama, and H. Yoshikawam. Modeling Design Processes. *AI Magazine*, pp. 37–48, Winter 1990.

[Ums90]   W. Umstätter. Informationslogistik: Distribution wissenschaftlicher Informationen. In B. Cronin and S. Klein (Eds.), *Informationsmanagement in Wissenschaft und Forschung*. Vieweg, Braunschweig, 1990.

[Vap95]   V. Vapnik. *The Nature of Statistical Learning Theory*. Springer, New York, 1995.

[VK04]   V. Vaishnavi and W. Kuechler. Design Research in Information Systems, July 2004. http://www.isworld.org/Researchdesign/drisISworld.htm. Retrieved May 9, 2005.

[vR79]   C. J. van Rijsbergen. *Information Retrieval*. Butterworth & Co (Publishers) Ltd., London, second edition, 1979.

[W3C99]   HTML 4.01 Specification. World WIde Web Consortium, December 1999. http://www.w3.org/TR/1999/REC-html401-19991224. Retrieved May 9, 2005.

[W3C02]   XML Signature Syntax and Processing. World Wide Web Consortium, February 2002. http://www.w3.org/TR/2002/REC-xmldsig-core-20020212/. Retrieved May 9, 2005.

[W3C04a]   OWL Web Ontology Language Overview. World Wide Web Consortium, February 2004. http://www.w3.org/TR/2004/REC-owl-features-20040210/. Retrieved May 9, 2005.

[W3C04b]   RDF Primer. World Wide Web Consortium, February 2004. http://www.w3.org/TR/2004/REC-rdf-primer-20040210/. Retrieved May 9, 2005.

[W3C04c]   RDF Vocabulary Description Language 1.0: RDF Schema. World Wide Web Consortium, February 2004. http://www.w3.org/TR/2004/REC-rdf-schema-20040210/. Retrieved May 9, 2005.

[W3C04d]   Resource Description Framework (RDF): Concepts and Abstract Syntax. World Wide Web Consortium, February 2004. http://www.w3.org/TR/2004/REC-rdf-concepts-20040210/. Retrieved May 9, 2005.

[W3C05]   SPARQL Query Language for RDF. World Wide Web Consortium, February 2005. http://www.w3.org/TR/2005/WD-rdf-sparql-query-20050217/. Retrieved February 28, 2005.

[WDB02]   M. Welsch, R. Dammers, and W. Bauer. IBM WebSphere Portal als Basis für Unternehmensportale. In S. Meinhardt and K. Popp (Eds.), *Enterprise-Portale & Enterprise Application Integration (HMD 225)*, Praxis der Wirtschaftsinformatik, pp. 31–41. dpunkt.verlag, Heidelberg, Germany, June 2002.

[Weg02]   C. Wege. Portal Server Technology. *IEEE Internet Computing*, 6(3), May/June 2002.

[WF00]   I. Witten and E. Frank. *Data Mining – Practical Machine Learning Tools and Techniques with Java Implementations*. Morgan Kaufmann Publishers, 2000.

[WG04]   M. Weisbrod and R. Ganser. *Microsoft Office SharePoint Portal Server 2003 – Das Handbuch*. Microsoft Press Deutschland, Unterschleißheim, 2004.

[Wii95]   K. M. Wiig. *Knowledge Management Methods*. Schema Press, Arlington, 1995.

[Wii99]   K. M. Wiig. Introducing Knowledge Management into the Enterprise. In J. Liebowitz (Ed.), *Knowledge Management Handbook*. CRC Press, Boca Raton, 1999.

[WL03]   Z. Wang and Q. Li. No Portal is an Island: Integrate Existing Applications into a Portal Framework. *WebSphere Developer's Journal*, 2(6), 2003. http://www.sys-con.com/WebSphere/articleprint.cfm?id=319. Retrieved May 9, 2005.